Once Upon a Time in Delhi

Author, editor and freelance journalist, Nita Berry has written short stories, picture and activity books, historical biographies, fiction and non-fiction for children of all ages, winning many awards for her writing, including the Shankar's Medal for Excellence in Writing. She was also part of NCERT's textbook development team that produced English readers for primary classes besides supplementary reading material.

Always fond of spinning a tale, Nita enjoyed writing from her earliest years in school and later at college. Living on a ship in the middle of nowhere as the wife of a master mariner, she wrote regularly for newspapers and magazines (including the iconic children's magazine *Target*), and created picture books for little readers. Nita also ran a children's centrespread in a weekly magazine and a bimonthly magazine for mariners' families. Currently, she looks after the publications of the Association of Writers and Illustrators for Children in New Delhi, and has represented India at several international conferences and workshops.

A homegrown Delhiwallah, she now lives with her family in Gurugram, but has not cut the cord with the eternal city. She believes that its chequered heritage will always belong to us all.

Once Upon a Time in Delhi

NITA BERRY

Illustrations by Mohit Suneja

hachette INDIA

First published in 2024 by Hachette India
(Registered name: Hachette Book Publishing India Pvt. Ltd)
An Hachette UK company
www.hachetteindia.com

SRD

Illustrations by Mohit Suneja
Images: Pages 219–20 are to be considered an extension of the copyright page.
Flower symbol by Aleks from Noun Project

ISBN: 978-93-5731-354-4

Hachette Book Publishing India Pvt. Ltd
4th & 5th Floors, Corporate Centre
Plot No. 94, Sector 44, Gurugram – 122003, India

Typeset by Manmohan Kumar, Delhi

Printed and bound in India
by Manipal Technologies Limited

MIX
Paper | Supporting responsible forestry
FSC™ C043100

For Aashira and Rivisha,
who may discover more secrets one day...

Contents

The Many Cities of Delhi

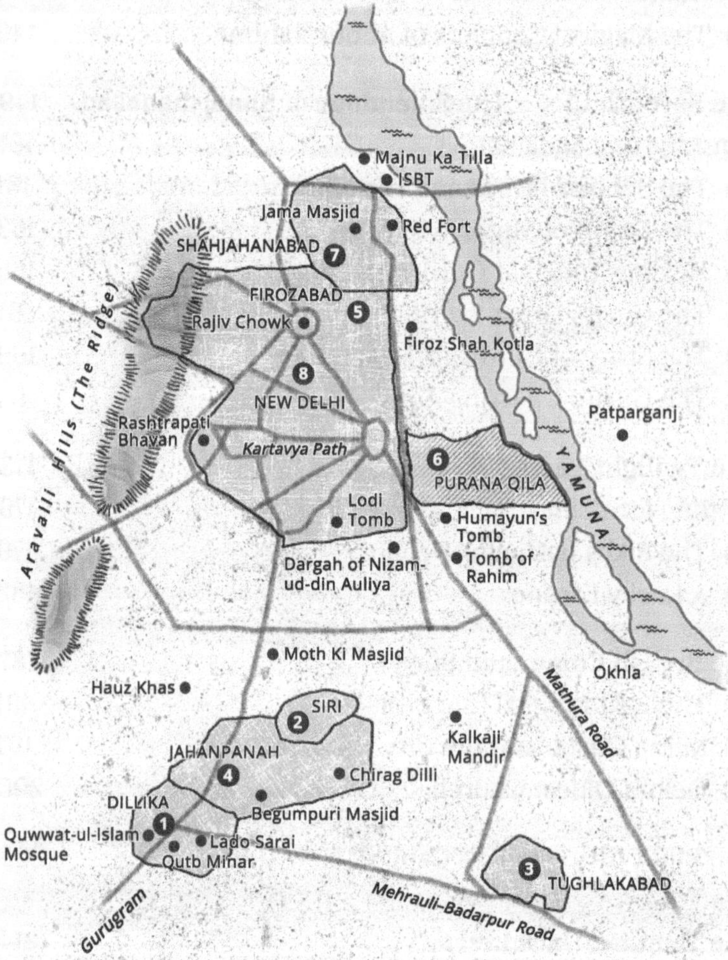

MAP NOT TO SCALE

Indraprastha

1. **Dillika:** 700–1290 CE
2. **Siri:** 1290–1320 CE
3. **Tughlakabad:** 1320–1325 CE
4. **Jahanpanah:** 1325–1351 CE
5. **Firozabad:** 1351–1388 CE
6. **Purana Qila:** 1533–1560 CE
7. **Shajahanabad:** 1633–1859 CE
8. **New Delhi:** 1911–Present

Let's Time Travel around Delhi

Imagine if you could board a time machine, hit the reverse button and...WHOOSH!

You would perhaps whizz past a blur of ancient cities if you stepped into Delhi, where our story is located – the splendid Shahjahanabad and the Purana Qila, past Firozabad, Jahanpanah and the sprawling Tughlakabad, and then all the way back to Siri and Dillika that stood here once upon a time. And what if you continued to travel further back in time? You might go back 3,000 years and beyond, to the legendary city of Indraprastha, the magnificent capital of the Pandavas, and even catch a glimpse of the epic battle of the Mahabharata – what a mind-blowing journcy that would bc!

Down the centuries there have been intrepid adventurers and invaders who, tempted to plunder the vast wealth of Delhi, crossed the mighty north-west Himalayas through narrow and treacherous passes. Others sought their fortunes in the city located strategically between the River Yamuna and the rocky Aravalli range. Standing at the crossroads of trade routes, it promised to be a gateway to the untold riches, power and culture of the fertile Indian plains.

Thus, Delhi became the battleground for bloody encounters, sieges and political intrigue. It suffered several shocks and underwent many changes in the course of its destiny as its many masters changed hands and it became the capital of almost a dozen mighty dynasties and empires. During medieval times, the city of Delhi changed location seven times altogether, within a triangle of about 200 square kilometres and with a different name each time. All these cities were always associated with imperial power and authority.

Delhi seems as old as time! Indeed, few places in the world are so steeped in history. It's probably the world's oldest capital city if one were to consider Indraprastha, which is said to have once stood here. Every niche and stone in the city has a tale to tell – of invasion and valour, violence and sacrifice. The eternal Yamuna that has flowed by this city down the ages, sometimes quiet, sometimes raging, is a witness to its glorious and tumultuous past.

Time machines, unfortunately, exist only in science fiction so far. Nonetheless, we can still uncover stories from the dim recesses of the past in an exciting journey through time, right here in these pages – gripping stories of kings and queens, saints, thugs and even djinns or ghosts who actually lived in the city!

Did you know...

... why Siri Fort was so named?

... that Delhi has the tallest brick minaret in the world?

... that it was once a walled city guarded by fourteen gates?

... that it has one of the oldest stadiums in India? And, ah yes –

... that butter chicken was first created in Delhi?

A historical thread running through this book strings together fascinating stories of each of the cities of Delhi.

But let's start at the very beginning to discover the amazing secrets of this unique city!

1

Before the Dawn of History

❁ An Epic Era ❁

The blind Kuru king of the Mahabharata, Dhritarashtra was in a royal quandary. His closest advisers were urging him to divide his kingdom into two parts – between the Kauravas, his beloved hundred sons, and the Pandavas, the five sons of his younger stepbrother, Pandu. Ever since Pandu's death in the forest, the princes had come to live with their uncle and the rest of the family, which included Bhishma, the family patriarch, and the other elders of the Kuru clan, in the prosperous capital city, Hastinapur.

A fierce rivalry broke out between the princes, and the Kauravas, especially Duryodhana, the eldest, became insanely jealous of their more accomplished cousins. They were especially envious of Bhima's physical strength and Arjuna's superb archery skills. What's more, the Pandavas were very popular with the people of Hastinapur who felt that Yudhishthira, the eldest Pandava prince, was the rightful heir to the throne. Duryodhana, colluding with his uncle, Shakuni, devised many devious plans, to kill his cousins. This eventually led to long years of hardship and exile for the Pandavas and their mother, Kunti.

Now, under pressure from Bhishma and from Dronacharya, who was the tutor of all the princes, Dhritarashtra divided his kingdom, cleverly making over the wild and uncultivable half to the Pandavas. Duryodhana would inherit the thriving part of the kingdom, which included Hastinapur. Yudhishthira accepted the dry and barren portion without protest and was later crowned king here.

The settlement that was the new home of the Pandavas was called Khandavaprastha, or a 'city of ruins'. It stood in a dense and thorny forest, which was the biggest of the five *prasthas* or 'plains' given to them by Dhritarashtra, the others being Sonaprastha, Paniprastha, Tilprastha and Bahakprastha (present-day Sonipat, Panipat, Tilpat, near Faridabad, and Baghpat). According to Dhritarashtra, this long-dead city was once the ancient capital of his ancestors, the Puruvas.

Desolate, overgrown and long-forgotten, Khandavaprastha was now a veritable ghost city inhabited only by birds and beasts, not to mention snakes and demons. The king of the snakes, Takshaka, was said to reign in this hilly, rocky terrain, protected by his friend, Indra, the king of the gods. Indra made sure to keep the land dry and barren so that no humans attempted to settle here.

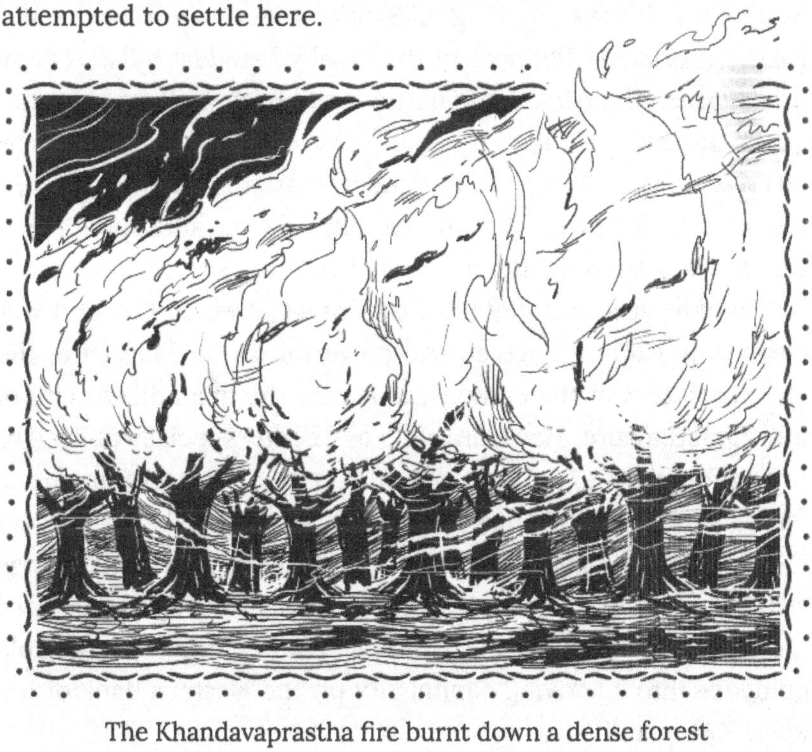

The Khandavaprastha fire burnt down a dense forest

This is the earliest reference to a settlement located in Delhi, which has been a seat of power even before the first millennium BCE. The Mahabharata goes on to narrate how Krishna and Arjuna resolved to set fire to the formidable Khandavaprastha forest and construct a splendid new city in its place. Aided by Agni, the god of fire, the conflagration is said to have raged for fifteen days, burning the forest to ashes and killing its creatures.

Father Fights Son

Indra, who was the father of Arjuna, now stepped in to stop the destruction of the jungle, which was under his protection. Summoning thunder and rain clouds, he frantically tried to quench the raging inferno. Arjuna shot his magical weapons to blow away Indra's clouds. Now, Indra hurled his most ferocious weapons at his son, making hailstones rain down from the sky. He even broke off the peak of the nearby Mandara hill and flung it at Arjuna. Their fearsome battle made both gods and mortals quake in terror. Ultimately, peace was restored with the timely intervention of Krishna. The Pandavas assured Indra that they would honour all who lived in Khandavaprastha and, appeased at last, Indra withdrew his curse from the land.

The darkness and gloom of the forest lifted as the land was cleared. Krishna requested the powerful *asura*, Mayasura, the chief architect of the demons, to create the magnificent city of Indraprastha here. Mayasura, who had been especially obliged to Arjuna for sparing his life during the terrible conflagration in the forest, was only too happy to do it.

And so, according to legend, Indraprastha was born. It was virtually a piece of heaven on earth, named in honour of Lord Indra. It soon developed and flourished under Yudhishthira's able guidance into a thriving capital city on the western bank of the River Yamuna.

Indraprastha was a city of unparalleled architectural marvels, as the Mahabharata tells us. The streets were wide and well laid out, with delightful gardens everywhere, and the new city stood adorned with palatial mansions and numerous gates. Priests, merchants and artisans flocked here, all eager to make it their new home.

The grandeur of Yudhishthira's palace drew gasps of admiration from all the visitors - sages, priests, kings and ministers - who were invited to his magnificent coronation ceremony. Columns of gold stood on floors that shone like water, while decorative pools inside the palace glittered like crystal. Not surprisingly, Indraprastha became the envy of the Kauravas, especially Duryodhana, for it was far grander than even Hastinapur, his capital.

The Mahabharata describes how Yudhishthira was lured into a game of dice with his Kaurava cousin, Duryodhana. He gambled away his entire kingdom, his wealth and even his wife, Draupadi! This ultimately led to the great war of annihilation, the epic battle of the Mahabharata, fought for the sake of Dharma on the plains of Kurukshetra, between the armies of the Pandavas and the Kauravas. Three generations lost their lives on this battlefield, which is said to have turned red with the blood shed over eighteen days. Only twelve warriors survived, including Lord Krishna and the five Pandavas.

After the devastating war, Yudhishthira mounted the golden throne of the Kurus, and became king of Indraprastha and Hastinapur. The city of Indraprastha retained its imperial grandeur throughout the epic era and was recognized as the backdrop for numerous legendary landmarks. Yudhishthira's reign here was said to be glorious and long, lasting thirty-six years, until he relinquished his throne and retired to the Himalayas with his brothers and Draupadi, on a long pilgrimage. He was succeeded by Pareekshit, son of the slain Pandava hero, Abhimanyu, and grandson of Arjuna. Yudhishthira appointed Yuyutsu, the only surviving son

The Mahabharata war

of Dhritarashtra, as his trusted regent, much as Bhishma had been for the Kauravas and the Pandavas. Pareekshit was succeeded by nearly thirty generations of his descendants. After this, Vishrava, a minister of the last king, Kshemaka, is said to have seized the throne for himself and established a new dynasty. Later dynasties were succeeded by the famous Mauryas of Magadha.

Ancient Indian literature tells us that Indraprastha was indeed a part of the Kuru kingdom. Buddhist texts in the Pali language also refer to the Kuru *mahajanapada*, with its capital at Indapatta, the Pali name for Indraprastha. Its strategic location on a major northern highway across the Gangetic plain made it a busy town, bustling with activity. Later, from the third century BCE, right up to the fifth century CE, Indraprastha and the area around it became part of the mighty Magadha and Gupta empires in ancient India. It also lay on the fringes of the Shunga Empire that ruled between these two great dynasties, from about 187 to 73 BCE. The magnificent old city thus lost much of its importance.

Over the centuries, Indraprastha faded into obscurity. The capital of the later Mauryan Empire was Pataliputra (now Patna), and Indraprastha was pushed to the backwoods. Much of its ancient history, therefore, finds no record, and this has been actually considered a lost period. Nevertheless, rural settlements always continued to exist here, including a village called 'Inderpat'.

Nothing remains of the city of Indraprastha today. Indeed, its story goes so far back into the mists of antiquity that the boundaries between mythology and history sometimes blur, and one is unsure where one ends and the other begins.

Indraprastha Comes Back to Life

Traditionally, the village Inderpat, which survived until the early twentieth century within Delhi's Purana Qila, was identified with Indraprastha. Interestingly, recent excavations within the Purana Qila revealed an area located on a mound between the Purana Qila and Humayun's Tomb, both of which were later constructed on the western banks of the Yamuna. This area has been found to have been occupied continuously since 1000 BCE. Archaeologists unearthed painted greyware (PGW) pottery, a style of fine, grey pottery painted with geometric patterns in black, dating back to 1000 BCE. Similar pottery has been discovered in other sites associated with the Mahabharata period too, such as Hastinapur near modern-day Meerut, Mathura and Kurukshetra. It seems to be typical of and related to this period. This, along with other ancient texts and inscriptions, has led historians to conclude that Yudhishthira's prosperous Indraprastha probably once stood at this site.

Exciting archaeological findings also tell us that the Purana Qila site has sediments and materials from various cultures, which have been deposited in successive layers over the last 3,000 years. Can you guess what the archaeologists have found? Earthen pottery articles, coins and glassware along with kiln-burnt bricks, terracotta toys and figurines, sickles and also ancient jewellery right from the Maurya era up to the later Shunga, Kushana, Gupta, Rajput, Sultanate and Mughal periods have been excavated. It is evident that the craftsmen were highly skilled here. Furthermore, images of various gods in exquisitely carved terracotta and soapstone from different periods have been unearthed during recent excavations. Clay was evidently used to make pots, and a potter's kiln, a brick kiln and a huge, brick platform have been found. Exquisite ornaments and amulets in various shapes appear to have been hewn from precious and semi-precious stones and ivory. Ongoing excavations have discovered beads made of various stones like jade, coral, crystal, agate and shell, and even a bone needle! Indeed, the old city has thrown up many surprises.

All these interesting finds have been displayed at the archaeological museum within the Purana Qila complex. They point to the existence of a rich and thriving culture here, and shed light on the historical significance and heritage of the area.

Taking us back to the misty past from the very heart of the capital today is perhaps Delhi's oldest monument: a splendid water reservoir rising from the deep depth of 60 feet to stand atop 108 stone steps. Agrasen Ki Baoli is an ancient stepwell

Agrasen Ki Baoli

believed to be built by the legendary Maharaja Agrasen of Agroha, an old town in today's Haryana, during the Mahabharata era. As Delhi lay in an arid belt bordering the desert, despite having the River Yamuna as its major water source, acute water shortages plagued the area since the earliest times. Besides, the monsoons have always been erratic in north India, so the necessity for water conservation was an integral part of life here. Stepwells were constructed ingeniously as water reservoirs, right from ancient times. The main users of these stairways were women. They collected the water and also prayed to the goddess of the well for her blessings. *Baolis* additionally served as a cool retreat for the local community during the hot summer months.

The rectangular Agrasen Ki Baoli was built over three levels in a unique architectural style with beautiful arched niches on all sides, using an intricate mosaic of stonework. These niches were used for rituals and religious ceremonies. Historical records say that the *baoli* was largely rebuilt in the fourteenth century during the Delhi Sultanate by the prosperous Agarwal community, who believed that they were direct descendants of Maharaja Agrasen of Agroha. The architectural style of the *baoli*, with its Tughlaq-era arches and arched niches, does indicate that it was rebuilt during the Tughlaq period.

This stepwell still stands on Hailey Road in the heart of the busy commercial area of Connaught Place, now known as Rajiv Chowk. It's in good shape even today and is a popular haunt for the local youth and for tourists. And, indeed, it is believed to be haunted! Spooky stories about the place abound.

The Delhi area was geographically significant as well, lying between the River Yamuna and a bustling trade route. According to historians, the recent discovery of over 136 coins and thirty-five seals belonging to different reigns during excavations in a small area at the Purana Qila site in January 2023 just goes to prove that there was much commercial activity in this prosperous area and that it had been inhabited continuously.

Today's Mathura Road, which runs past the Purana Qila, is a part of the Grand Trunk Road built by Sher Shah Suri in the sixteenth century. It was one of the longest and oldest roads in Asia, roughly 3,710 km long, and spanned from Kabul in Afghanistan to Teknaf in present-day Bangladesh. Over the centuries, this highway acted as one of the major trade routes in the region.

Ongoing archaeological excavations at the site promise to uncover the deepest mysteries beneath the Purana Qila complex. Perhaps the assortment of jigsaw pieces will be put together before very long to give us a more complete picture of the past!

Discovering Indraprastha

The destinies of the cities of Indraprastha and Hastinapur were closely intertwined, ruled as they were by the Kuru dynasty. The Kauravas and the Pandavas all belonged to this ancient dynasty. The deadly battle between them was fought on the plains of Kurukshetra, which means 'place of Kuru', or King Kuru, their great ancestor. There is a prologue to this enthralling saga.

Ganga's Gift

The Mahabharata narrates how thousands of years ago, the grandfather of the Kauravas and the Pandavas, Raja Shantanu, the Kuru king of Hastinapur, was out hunting when a beautiful damsel on the banks of the River Ganga captivated him instantly. Asking her curiously who she was, he entreated her to marry him and be his queen.

Smiling mysteriously, she replied, 'O, Great King! I will marry you and live in your palace, but on one condition alone - never ask me who I am or question what I do. And treat me well - otherwise I will go away.'

The king agreed readily, and they were happily married. In the course of time, the queen gave birth to seven beautiful sons. As soon as each was born, she carried the baby to the river

King Shantanu is perplexed by Ganga's actions

and threw him into the water. Raja Shantanu was horrified but helpless because of his promise.

When the eighth son was born, he could contain himself no longer. 'Stop!' he cried, blocking the queen's path to the river. 'O Heartless One, why do you kill our sons thus?'

Unmoved, the queen replied, 'Since you have broken your promise, O King, I will leave you now. But let me explain. I am the goddess Ganga. These eight sons were the eight Vasus who wished to be born to me on earth, because they were cursed by Sage Vashishtha. They had to be thrown into the river to be liberated from his curse. However, the eighth Vasu will have to spend his entire life on earth. I will bring him up and return him to you when he is older.'

And so it was. The eighth Vasu, Gangadatta (or 'Ganga's gift'), grew up to become Devavrata, the beloved son and heir apparent of Raja Shantanu. Years later, to enable his father to marry Satyavati, the daughter of a fisherman, he renounced his claim to the throne and even vowed never to marry. Blessed by the gods, he was renamed 'Bhishma' because of his firm commitment to lifelong celibacy. In the course of time, Bhishma Pitamah became the great patriarch of the Kuru clan - the Kauravas, and the Pandavas who would create the magnificent capital city of Indraprastha.

Father of a Hundred Sons

The eldest of the heirs to the Kuru throne, Dhritarashtra was born blind, according to the Mahabharata. So, his younger brother, Pandu, ascended the throne of Hastinapur.

Bhishma brought up the two princes, who were the grandsons of Raja Shantanu and Satyavati, as his own children. When they were old enough, he began to look for suitable wives for them. He had learnt that Gandhari, the daughter of King Subala of

Gandhara, had received a boon from Lord Shiva that she would bear a hundred sons. So he sent a messenger to King Subala, asking for her hand in marriage for Dhritarashtra.

Gandhari married him willingly despite knowing that Dhritarashtra was blind. What is more, she vowed to share the darkness he lived in, stating, 'I do not wish to see the world that my husband cannot see.' It is said that she tied a piece of silk over her eyes for the rest of her life.

Strangely enough, after two years, Gandhari gave birth not to a hundred sons as prophesied, but to a hard mass of lifeless flesh. Horrified, she was about to throw it away, when Rishi Vyas appeared and directed her to arrange for a hundred jars of ghee. He began to carve the lump of flesh into one hundred small pieces. Each, he said, would develop inside a jar into a son. Gandhari promptly begged the sage for a daughter as well. Rishi Vyas agreed and, accordingly, cut the lump of flesh into a hundred and one pieces. He placed each piece in a jar, saying that these would be ready to be opened after two more years. All the jars were stowed away into a dark cave.

And so, after two more years, a hundred sons and one daughter were produced from each of the jars. The hundred sons of Dhritarashtra came to be known as the Kauravas. Dushala was their only sister. Duryodhana was the first born, and Dhritarashtra loved him dearly. It was indeed his blind love for his son that led to ultimate calamity.

The epic, the Mahabharata, is a remarkable story of ambition and intrigue, heroism and Dharma, culminating in an eighteen-day battle on the plains of Kurukshetra, about 130 kilometres from Indraprastha. Kurukshetra was a part of Kuru territory. It was regarded as a *dharmakshetra* or holy land. Anyone dying on this plain would go to heaven, according to a boon granted to King Kuru by Vishnu. Practically the entire clan – except for the five Pandavas, was annihilated here. It is said that so much blood flowed that the battlefield at Kurukshetra turned red as the two conflicting armies, the Kauravas and the Pandavas slaughtered each other ruthlessly.

It was during this great battle that the *Bhagavad Gita*, or the Song Divine, was delivered by Lord Krishna, the divine charioteer of Arjuna, who urged him to do his duty without fear or attachment to its consequences. This revered 700-verse Hindu scripture is one of the gems of the Mahabharata and teaches one how to live a spiritual and successful life.

Here too at Kurukshetra, towards the end of the gruesome war, the great patriarch of the Kuru clan, Bhishma Pitamah, who was the commander-in-chief of the Kaurava army, lay on the battlefield, riddled with arrows. He is said to have waited patiently for fifty-eight nights for the onset of the auspicious *Uttarayana*, or winter solstice, on Makar Sankranti, to give up his body. As he lay stretched on his bed of arrows, surrounded by the Pandavas, Draupadi and Krishna, Yudhishthira questioned him closely about the path of peace, virtue and faith. The mighty warrior's reply forms the ancient prayer, the Vishnu Sahasranam, which is widely recited even today.

On the basis of planetary positions recorded in the Mahabharata and literary evidence from Puranic and Vedic texts, the date derived for the actual occurrence of the Kurukshetra war is 3100 BCE.

The Miracle of Yogmaya

The Yogmaya Temple in the heart of Mehrauli is said to be as ancient as the Mahabharata itself, and almost as old as Yudhisthira's capital city of Indraprastha. The temple's main idol is believed to be that of Lord Krishna's sister, Yogmaya.

Krishna was said to have been born in the prison of Mathura. His parents, Vasudeva and Devki, knew that Devki's brother, Kansa, the cruel ruler of Mathura, terrified by a divine prophesy that he would meet his end at the hands of Devki's eighth son, would want to kill the baby, just as he had killed the seven others born to her earlier.

Legend tells us that when Krishna was born, the prison filled with divine light. The prison guards fell into a deep slumber and the doors opened miraculously. Vasudeva escaped from the prison with the newborn baby hidden in a wicker basket and rushed to Gokul, on the opposite bank of the Yamuna. He crossed the river during a raging storm to reach the house of the cowherd, Nanda, and his wife, Yashoda. It is said that the Yamuna parted its turbulent waters to make way for Vasudeva. Baby Krishna was swiftly exchanged for Yashoda's baby girl, Yogmaya, and Vasudeva rushed back to Mathura, to place the tiny girl next to Devki.

The next morning, hearing of the birth of Devki's eighth child, Kansa rushed into the prison cell to kill the baby. Paying no heed to his sister's pleas to spare the tiny girl, he was about to smash the baby's head heartlessly against a stone slab, when the girl vanished into thin air. Only a voice echoed, 'Kansa, your slayer is born and is safe!'

This was the miracle of Yogmaya or 'divine illusion'. Many years later, Kansa would meet his death at the hands of the young Krishna in a fierce contest.

The Pandavas are believed to have built the Yogmaya Temple, dedicated to Goddess Yogmaya, after their victory at Kurukshetra. Ancient Jain scriptures sometimes refer to the Mehrauli area as Yoginipura, or 'fortress of female divinities', which was probably named after the temple of this goddess. Indeed, in several parts of India, Yogmaya is worshipped as *shakti* or female power.

However, the Yogmaya Temple is the only one of its kind dedicated to Goddess Yogmaya. It was first renovated during the rule of the Mughal emperor, Akbar Shah II, in the nineteenth century, by Lala Sethmal. An interesting story is told about the Queen Mumtaz Mahal II. In 1808, her son, Prince Mirza Jahangir, had fired at the British Resident, Archibald Seton, from the

Red Fort, resulting in the death of the latter's bodyguard. Bent on avenging the insult, the Resident returned with a group of British troops, arrested the prince and exiled him to Allahabad (now Prayagraj).

The queen was deeply distraught at the imprisonment and exile of her favourite son and prayed for his safe return. Goddess Yogmaya appeared to the queen in a dream, after which Mumtaz Mahal vowed to place a flower fan or *pankha* at the Yogmaya Temple in Mehrauli, as also in the nearby *dargah* of the great thirteenth-century Sufi saint, Khwaja Bakhtiyar Kaki, if her son returned safely. Prince Mirza Jahangir was released and sent back to Delhi after the British relented. The overjoyed queen kept her promise, and so began the tradition of offering a floral *pankha* and canopy at the Yogmaya Temple, and a *chaadar* at the shrine of Bakhtiyar Kaki in a procession every year, to the accompaniment of drummers and *shehnai* players.

This tradition continues to this day in the name of Phoolwalon Ki Sair, a unique flower festival meaning 'procession of florists'. It is held for three days in October every year, to celebrate the spirit of communal harmony. Phoolwalon Ki Sair wends its way through Mehrauli, led by dancers and *shehnai* players in brocade sherwanis, towards the *dargah* of Khwaja Bakhtiyar Kaki. Cultural troupes from various Indian states perform dances and plays at Jahaz Mahal in Mehrauli, which is shaped like a ship and located in a corner of the Hauz-i-Shamsi, raising the festival beyond the original vision of communal harmony to that of national integration.

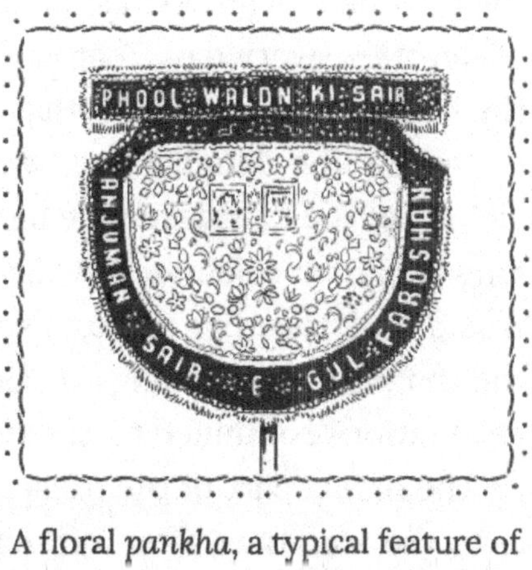

A floral *pankha*, a typical feature of the Phoolwalon Ki Sair procession

Interestingly, to this day, the ancient Yogmaya Temple

and its deity are cared for by the descendants of its caretakers from the days of the Mahabharata.

The Ancient Kalkaji Temple

It is believed from early times that two goddesses protected Delhi – Yogmaya and Kali Devi.

The Mahabharata tells us that after their victory in the war, the Pandavas travelled around with Lord Krishna and built five temples as thanksgiving. They are said to have visited the Suryakoot hill of the ancient Aravalli range, believed to be the birthplace of Goddess Kali in Delhi's present-day Kalkaji area, and built a temple here to the goddess. They also prayed to her for power, strength and resilience.

The history of this ancient temple, which is believed to be over 3,000 years old, goes even further back into time, for it is known as the place where Goddess Kali manifested herself in a fearful battle with giant demons who had terrorized the local gods. After she destroyed the dreaded enemies, she settled down here and was worshipped as the chief deity. Kalkaji Temple is believed to be the holy shrine where the goddess blesses one for the fulfilment of all desires. To this day, it is visited by thousands of devotees every day. That is why the temple is also known as the Manokamna Siddha Peetha.

During the Mughal era, *dharamshalas* were built in the vicinity of the Kalkaji Temple by nobles. Huge Navaratri *melas* or fairs would be celebrated twice a year by all communities, who would walk together through sprawling mustard fields towards the temple, singing songs to Goddess Kali Devi. These festive celebrations continued till the twentieth century.

The oldest part of the present temple was built around 1764 CE by the Marathas, after Aurangzeb had destroyed much of the ancient temple. Mirza Raja Kidarnath, the treasurer of the Mughal king, Akbar Shah II, also added his own modifications about fifty years later. The existing temple took shape in the early twentieth century. Today, the Kalkaji Temple, with its thirty-six arched entrances, stands near the bustling commercial hub of Nehru Place, Kalkaji Mandir Metro Station and the Lotus Temple – a far cry indeed from the ancient battleground of demons, gods and goddesses!

A Teacher and 105 Students – Gurukul to Gurugram!

Gurugram, or 'teacher's village', lay on the hot and dusty plains, a short distance away from Indraprastha, the Mahabharata tells us. It is said to have existed even before Yudhishthira built his magnificent city. This was the *ashram* village of Guru Dronacharya, the son of Rishi Bharadwaj, who tutored the Pandavas and their cousins, the Kauravas, in the martial arts at his *gurukul* or residence. The village was believed to have been gifted to the revered guru as *gurudakshina* by Yudhishthira, the eldest of the Pandavas, and it developed into a centre of learning.

Late in the fourth century BCE, along with Indraprastha, the small village of Gurugram was absorbed by the Mauryan Empire as part of Chandragupta Maurya's earliest expansion of his kingdom. Later still, it came under Rajput rule, right until the twelfth century, when Muhammad Ghori's conquest of Delhi also included this ancient settlement. The destiny of the entire area then changed, and it lay in the shadow of the many dynasties that ruled from the imperial capital of Delhi.

In the fourteenth century, a Moroccan scholar called Ibn Battuta travelled extensively throughout Asia, Africa, India and Europe, and spent many years here in the Tughlaq Empire. He wrote about a structure of Islamic importance at a place near Delhi, on the way to Ajmer. This was Gurugram, which was on the caravan route linking Delhi to Ajmer through Jaipur, and it was an important trading junction for goods in the dry belt, south of Delhi. Over the centuries, it developed as a major market for agricultural commodities like jaggery and several varieties of food grains.

In those faraway days, when long journeys through this arid belt were undertaken on foot or with the use of draught animals, *piaos* or refreshment halts were often constructed on well-trodden routes. These provided water and a place of rest for travellers, pilgrims and traders, and those whose lives were spent on the road. A few ancient *piaos* made of brick, with umbrella-like canopies that afford shade and ventilation, still survive, standing at a short distance from Gurugram in the Jhajjar and Bhiwani districts. They were probably built by the business community of those times.

Ancient *piao* at Jhajjar

Later, with the decline of the Mughal Empire, the area was torn between many contending powers. By the nineteenth century, it had come under British rule. After Indian independence in 1947, Gurugram fell under the Indian state of Punjab, and almost two decades later, the city became part of the new state of Haryana.

For many decades known popularly as Gurgaon and forming a part of the National Capital Region, the city regained its ancient name only in 2016. Gurugram has grown rapidly from a sleepy town to a fast-paced urban centre and a thriving suburb of New Delhi. The Millennium City, as it is often called today, is a leading financial and industrial hub for large business houses, professionals and multinational companies.

The Legend of Drona

Who was Guru Dronacharya from whom Gurugram takes its name?

An intriguing story in the Mahabharata tells us how Drona became the guru of the young Kaurava and Pandava princes in Hastinapur. They were playing with a ball when it bounced high and fell into a well. They could not retrieve it despite their best efforts and peered despairingly down into its dark depths.

A young, dark-skinned brahmin watched with some amusement from afar. 'Young princes, you are all *kshatriyas* and skilled archers, but cannot even recover a ball from a well!' he teased, coming up to them. 'If you promise me dinner, I shall bring up not only your ball but also this ring, which I'll throw in... Now, just watch me!' And saying this, he took off his ring and tossed it into the well.

The young man grabbed a fistful of reeds and, chanting softly, threw one reed effortlessly into the well where it pierced the ball that was bobbing on the water. He then threw in a second stalk which pierced the first reed, and then a third, until a long chain was formed. He pulled up the chain of reeds and the ball emerged. The princes gaped in astonishment. Never had such a feat been witnessed before! Next, he shot an arrow into the water. It pierced his ring and rebounded with it.

Bhishma, the patriarch of the Kuru clan was deeply impressed by what the excited princes told him. 'Such an extraordinary one can only be Drona, the son of the sage Bharadwaja, and one of the greatest archers in the world. He is said to have learned archery from the gods themselves! I will bring him to the palace myself and entreat him to be your teacher.'

And so it was. Drona became the great guru of the Kaurava and Pandava princes at Hastinapur and trained them in the art of archery.

Local folklore tells us that the *gurukul* of Guru Dronacharya came up later in his ancestral village, named Gurugram or Gurgaon in recent times. His young students, the Kaurava and

Guru Dronacharya and his royal students

Pandava princes, were trained in archery and the other martial arts when they lived here. The popular Sheetala Mata Temple in the vicinity is said to be named after Dronacharya's wife, Kripi, later known as Mata Sheetala Devi. She is a popular deity in Gurugram today, believed to cure all kinds of illnesses.

The Delhi Metro has paid rich tribute to the legendary warrior Drona, as its first halt in Gurugram is called 'Guru Dronacharya Metro Station', named after this venerable guru of the Kurus.

Arjuna and Dronacharya

Dronacharya was a stern and exacting teacher who frequently put his students to test in his *gurukul* in Gurugram.

'Tell me, what do you see, Yudhishthira?' he asked one day. 'Do you see the eye of the bird?'

'*Guruji*, I see the pigeon, the tree, the clouds...' replied Yudhishthira eagerly, aiming his arrow at the clay pigeon on the tree.'

Dronacharya shook his head, deeply disappointed. 'You may go, Yudhishthira. You have not learned enough.'

He went on to ask each of the Pandava and Kaurava princes the same question, and each time he received the same reply.

Finally, it was Arjuna's turn. When Dronacharya asked him what he saw, he replied, 'I see nothing but the pigeon's eye.'

Dronacharya's eyes gleamed with pleasure. 'Describe the pigeon, Arjuna,' he urged.

'I see no pigeon, only its eye,' Arjuna repeated.

'Shoot!' commanded Dronacharya. The next moment, Arjuna's arrow shot the clay pigeon's eye, and its head tumbled down to the ground.

'You are a true archer!' Dronacharya embraced Arjuna joyfully. 'The archer sees nothing but his target. Nobody will ever surpass you in archery. You will be invincible!'

And indeed, Arjuna went on to become Dronacharya's greatest pupil...even though there could well have been somebody else!

The Gurudakshina of Eklavya

The Nishada tribal chief's son had a dream. He fervently wanted to be the greatest archer in the world. To achieve this, he needed a great guru like Drona to teach him.

Many years ago, he had asked Drona to accept him as his disciple, but Drona had curtly refused. He taught only *kshatriyas*, he said. The Nishadas were tribal hunters who lived on the fringe of society.

Eklavya, the young tribal boy, never lost heart all those years. He made a clay image of Drona in the forest where he lived near Dronacharya's *gurukul* in Gurugram, and drawing inspiration from this, diligently mastered the bow and arrow.

The princes were on a hunting expedition in this forest when their dog started barking furiously. An unknown archer shot seven quick arrows into its mouth to silence it, without causing any injury. The young princes were astounded to see their dog return with a mouthful of arrows.

They began hunting for the skilled archer and met Eklavya. He was honoured and delighted. 'I am Dronacharya's disciple, Eklavya,' he bowed, introducing himself.

Arjuna went back to the ashram and complained bitterly to Dronacharya. 'You had promised to make me the greatest archer in the world, but you have another pupil who is even better than I am!' He led his puzzled teacher into the forest where Eklavya was practising with his bow and arrow.

When Eklavya saw Dronacharya, he immediately ran forward and touched his feet. Dronacharya asked him who he was. When the boy had told him his story, Dronacharya immediately remarked, 'You are my disciple, so you must pay me *gurudakshina*.'

'Of course, Guru-ji!' Eklavya exclaimed fervently, his eyes shining. 'There is nothing I shall not give you happily!'

'Then give me your right thumb.'

Eklavya's reverence for his guru was unmatched. He cut off his thumb unhesitatingly and handed it to Dronacharya. Arjuna was stunned – but relieved. He and Dronacharya both knew then that nobody could equal Arjuna, the archer.

Today, a small temple called Eklavya Mandir stands in Khandsa village near Gurugram's Hero Honda Chowk, where this entire incident is said to have taken place. It is believed that Eklavya's thumb lies buried here. This temple is supposed to have been built during Mahabharata times – the only one in the country dedicated to the skilled tribal archer.

Timeline:
8 BCE–1290 CE

2

The First City
Dillika Is Born

Discovering Dillika

After the decay of Indraprastha, nothing was known about a city in this location for many centuries. According to legend, the city of Dilli, which came up here afterwards, is believed to have gotten its name in the eighth century BCE from Raja Dhilu, who was said to belong to the Jat Dhillon dynasty. However, modern historians credit him to be a later king of the Mauryan dynasty in the first century BCE. So there are conflicting accounts of the timeline of Delhi, but all agree that Raja Dhilu built a township on the plains of Yoginipura near the ancient Yogmaya Temple in Mehrauli and renamed it after himself. While the exact origin of the name 'Delhi' as we know it is unknown, the various names the city has been known by – Dilli, Dillika, Dhilli, Dehli and Delhi – are thought to be subsequent corruptions of his name.

The fortunes of this ancient city underwent many adverse changes after the reign of Raja Dhilu and it became hidden in the mists of history again for the next nine or ten centuries. The capital of the Gangetic plains had shifted eastwards to Pataliputra with the establishment of the mighty Magadha, Mauryan and Gupta empires between the sixth century BCE and the sixth century CE, and Delhi lay largely deserted except for clusters of rural settlements.

The Rajputs had become increasingly powerful in northern India from the eighth century onwards. The name Rajput came from *raja-putra* in Sanskrit, meaning 'son of a king'. This brave warrior community claimed descent from ruling Hindu warrior classes or *kshatriyas*. Divided into thirty-six clans, they reigned in north and north-western India, the major Rajput dynasties being the Pratiharas of Kannauj, the Parmars of Malwa, the Chauhans of Ajmer and the Chalukyas of Kathiawar, besides many others. Stories abound of their valour and their fearless queens. There could be nothing more dishonourable for a Rajput than to run away from the battlefield. If widowed, their valiant women would rather die than face disgrace at the hands of the enemy.

The Tomar Rajputs were said to be descendants of the Pandavas. It was only in the eighth century CE that Dillika, the first of the seven medieval cities of Delhi, was founded on the ruins of Raja Dhilu's ancient city by Anangapala I, chief of the Tomar Rajputs who ruled the neighbouring Haryana region in the Aravalli hills. He laid the foundation of Dillika as the capital of several villages in and around Hariyanika or 'abode of God' in today's Delhi–Haryana region. We know all this from inscriptions, coins and folklore as passed down the generations, and this is where recorded history actually begins.

Anangapala and his successors, the Tomar kings, reigned here generally undisturbed for a century, although there were conflicts with neighbours. During this time, they were able to construct the city walls as well as many structures, dams and tanks. Anangapala II built the majestic city of Dillika in red stone, and it stretched from present-day Lado Sarai to Mehrauli. It boasted of a citadel called the Lal Kot or Red Fortress, which had strongly fortified walls with bastions. This was probably an effective deterrent against the designs of other Rajput clans. The famous Iron Pillar of Mehrauli was also probably brought here from Udayagiri in Madhya Pradesh and installed by Anangapala II in the main Tomar Temple. Indeed, the pillar has a short inscription that mentions both him and the city of Dillika.

Dillika lay in an arid belt bordering the Rajasthan desert, and it suffered from acute water shortages. This necessitated the construction of stepwells or *baolis*, which harvested rainwater for water sources for the locals. Far back in time, the Agrasen Ki Baoli had come up as a necessity in the parched land. Anangapala II built the Anangatal Baoli behind the Yogmaya Temple, in a dense forest in Mehrauli. This large, single-stage stepwell went down about 45 feet deep and, apart from being a water reservoir, it was believed to be the site of annual almsgiving events held by the queens of the time.

The many Rajput clans fought each other constantly through the eleventh and twelfth centuries. The Tomar clan was overtaken in the twelfth century by the Chauhans when Prithviraj Chauhan, the heroic warrior king of Ajmer, inherited Dillika from his maternal grandfather, Anangapala II.

Fascinated by the many charms of Dillika, Prithviraj made it his capital city. He enlarged the fortress of Lal Kot by building massive ramparts with thirteen gates, called the Qila Rai Pithora, around the city, totalling a circumference of about 8 kilometres.

However, Prithviraj's was a short and torrid existence. He resisted a fierce attack by the Turk invader, Muhammad Ghori, at Tarain, near today's Karnal; but after his subsequent defeat and death in 1192 CE, the road to Delhi lay open to attack and invasion.

Like many waves of invaders and traders before them, Muhammad Ghori's forces came through the mountain passes of the rugged north-west frontier to reach the plains of India. He himself belonged to a Turkish tribe but had moved eastwards to establish himself as master of Ghor located in Afghanistan.

The throne of Delhi now passed to Muhammad Ghori. With his victory over Prithviraj Chauhan, the Rajput fort, Lal Kot, fell into the hands of the invading army. This was a major turning point in the history of the city, as indeed in Indian history. Delhi would remain under Muslim rule for the next 700 years until 1857, and then under British rule right until Indian independence in 1947.

However, Ghor in Afghanistan was under constant attack. So, Muhammad Ghori entrusted his general, Qutbuddin Aibak, with

The assassination of Muhammad Ghori

the task of the consolidation and expansion of his Indian conquests, and returned to Afghanistan, laden with spoils. It is believed that he was murdered on his way back in 1206.

It was a curious turn of events! Qutbuddin, who remained in India, declared himself sultan of Delhi and Muhammad Ghori's territories in northern India and occupied the Rajput fort. This was the beginning of the Delhi sultanate.

It was the beginning too of the so-called 'Slave' dynasty, so named because its three most powerful rulers – Qutbuddin, Iltutmish and Balban – were all former slaves, having been bought and sold in their early lives. With time, they proved their military and organizational skills to become trusted generals. They were released from slavery and ultimately succeeded their masters. No longer referred to as the 'Slave' dynasty, it is now known as the dynasty of the Ilbari Turks as all its rulers, except Qutbuddin, were Turks belonging to the Ilbari tribe. And only three of the nine sultans had been slaves at one time.

Qutbuddin was an enthusiastic builder. He celebrated his victory by erecting the Quwwat-ul-Islam Mosque, meaning 'might of Islam', in Mehrauli. It was a symbol of the might of a new political power.

We should thank the Delhi sultanate, especially Qutbuddin Aibak for bringing us kebabs, according to Ibn Battuta, the Moroccan traveller. It is said that soldiers of the Ottoman Empire (modern day Turkey) were given spiced minced meat by their wives before going to battle. That is how this hot delicacy originated before it was brought to the Indian subcontinent!

More than twenty-five temples were said to have existed here from the time of the Pandavas right up to the reign of the Chauhans. Their pillars, arches, slabs and other structural parts were reused by the new rulers, and the original images were plastered over. Carved Hindu motifs on salvaged and recycled masonry can be found today throughout the mosque, in combination with Islamic arabesque patterns and Quranic inscriptions.

The Quwwat-ul-Islam was the first mosque to be raised in India by a ruling dynasty and is considered a masterpiece of Indo-Islamic architecture, which blends Indian and Islamic styles. Islamic structures adapted the skills of workers in local traditions to their own designs.

Near the mosque, the sultan began the construction of the famous Qutb Minar in red sandstone and marble – a monumental tower of victory to herald his rule in India. However, his reign lasted only four years and he could build only a single-storeyed *minar*. The ground storey was constructed over the ruins of Lal Kot, the citadel of Dillika. His clever and capable son-in-law, Shamsuddin Iltutmish, the governor of Badayun, succeeded him and added three more storeys to the Qutb Minar, making it the towering structure it was meant to be. This conspicuous 73-metre-high landmark of the capital city stands tall even today and is the country's highest stone tower.

Later, in 1369, the Qutb Minar's topmost storey was damaged by lightning and was rebuilt by Firoz Shah Tughlak – who ruled the Delhi sultanate three dynasties and fifteen sultans later, from 1351 to 1388, and added yet another storey to the *minar*. This is one of the reasons why the fluted tower has a varied architectural façade, ranging from the time of Qutbuddin to that of the Tughlak dynasty.

Iltutmish did not consider any of his sons worthy of the prestigious throne of Delhi. Before he died, contrary to custom, he decided to make his daughter his successor to the throne. The annals of history had never before seen such an extraordinary

decision! And so, Razia Sultana became the only queen ever to sit on the throne of Delhi. The new queen was able and just, but many of her generals resented a woman ruler and soon had her killed. This marked the beginning of the end of the dynasty of the Ilbari Turks.

Those were turbulent times indeed! Confusion reigned until Balban took over the administration of Delhi with a firm hand. He had been bought as a slave by Iltutmish, and was the chief minister of his grandson, Nasiruddin Mahmud. Balban was indeed the most powerful ruler of the Delhi sultanate, after Iltutmish. However, his weak descendants were overthrown in 1290 CE by the Khiljis, who came from Afghanistan and wrested the throne of Delhi. Like the Ilbari Turks, the Khiljis too were Turks, but had been long settled in Afghanistan.

The defeat of the Rajputs had thus drastically changed the fortunes and very essence of Delhi. The Delhi sultanate became a magnet for Turks from central and western Asia, Persia and Afghanistan. Most of the ruling class as well as the cultural elite were Turks.

For the people of Dillika, the arrival of the Turks and the establishment of the Delhi sultanate was a period of both turmoil and development. However, once they had submitted to their new conquerors, a process of peace slowly started. The Muslim invaders brought with them many new ways of life and thought in every sphere – like religion, language, food, customs, mannerisms, architecture and culture – so there was some give and take; and the Muslims in turn were influenced by the local customs and culture of their new country. Development in these fields became important milestones in the growth of a composite culture.

The city's rich Hindu-Jain-Buddhist heritage was influenced by the new ways of its conquerors, although their social life remained relatively unchanged. The majority of them were vegetarian, as were most Sufis and their followers, whereas Turkish cuisine was largely non-vegetarian. However, some customs concerning food, clothing, music and art were adapted by both sides. All sorts of clothes in silk, wool and cotton were used by everyone as were ornaments of gold and silver and precious stones. Fairs and religious festivals were common entertainment for all communities.

The *paan*, or betel leaf, soon became popular with the ruling class and the use of local spices transformed many of their dishes such as pilau. They also adopted Indian headgear and many of their ceremonies, especially those related to marriage and death, showed great local influence. Local music also made its impact on them, resulting in the emergence of a new kind of music in north India, such as *qawwali*.

The popular betel leaf or paan

With the arrival of the Turks, a new language, Persian, was introduced to the country. Right from the start, it was adopted as the language of literature and administration here. The destruction of the cultural centres of Central and West Asia by the Mongols had led many scholars and poets to take refuge in the Delhi sultanate. And so, Delhi became the most important cultural hub in the East. These distinguished refugees were welcomed by sultans like Balban and given high offices in the court. Even so, Sanskrit continued to be a vehicle of higher thought and philosophy, and poetry and drama were written in Sanskrit. The Jains too contributed to the growth of Sanskrit.

In architecture, architects from Central Asia brought with them Turkish traditions like creating lotus bud fringes on the underside of arches. On the other hand, the influence of Hindu Rajput craftsmen is visible in the naturalistic motifs, the serpentine tendrils and even the curve of the letters of Koranic inscriptions in the new Islamic structures. The skill of the Indian stonecutters and sculptors was used here, as also the addition of contrasting colours to these buildings using marble and red and yellow sandstone, which was a local concept in the subcontinent. These were the beginnings of a rich, syncretic culture in every domain.

Intricate inlay work in marble

The sultans also adopted the ancient Hindu practice of constructing stepwells or *baolis* in the arid belt they had chosen to settle in. Water reservoirs like Gandhak Ki Baoli and Rajon Ki Baoli, then tucked away in the narrow lanes of Mehrauli amid thick forests, stand today as forgotten legacies of the sultans.

With the coming of Islam to India came their mystics, the venerable Sufi saints. These mystics rejected religious rituals, stressing on love and intense devotion as a means of reaching the Almighty. They composed devotional poems on their longing for oneness with God, invoking the divine presence through song and music. They lived spiritual, disciplined lives in their *khanqahs*, or monasteries, detached from material pleasures.

Several Sufi shrines came up in Delhi in the thirteenth and fourteenth centuries, giving the city a unique sanctity. These sites became places of pilgrimage for people of all faiths, as also centres of music, culture and philosophy. Settlements developed around them, and the city of Delhi often came to be known by the title of these revered Sufi saints, as 'Hazrat Dehli'. Great saints like Qutbuddin Bakhtiyar Kaki, Nizamuddin Auliya and Chirag-e-Dehlavi made the city their home. They were influenced by the local environment, ideas and philosophy; and they in turn undoubtedly inspired the saints of the later Bhakti movement here, which emerged against rituals and caste barriers. For the Bhakti saints, God was supreme, all people were equal in His eyes and devotion to Him was the only way to achieve salvation. Later religious movements like Sikhism also had some elements of the Bhakti movement.

The ruins of Dillika may be seen scattered around the Mehrauli area and in the Qutb complex even today. Along with the ancient Anangatal Baoli, the original fort of Lal Kot lies inside Sanjay Van – a huge forest with indigenous medicinal trees and plants between Mehrauli and Vasant Kunj – now mostly in ruins. Its stone ramparts and the remains of a moat continue to stand only in a few places.

All that remains of the walls of the Qila Rai Pithora is scattered across south Delhi, and is visible in Saket, Mehrauli, around the Qutb complex, Vasant Kunj and Kishangarh. Only three gates of the fort remain – the imposing Badayun Gate, which once was the main entrance to the city of Dillika, along with the Hauz Rani and Barka gates. The remains of the Badayun Gate lie within the Qila Rai Pithora grounds of the Lado Sarai Golf Course on Press Enclave Road. Close by, the Rai Pithora Cultural Complex is a lush heritage park with walking trails, run by the Delhi administration. In addition to a museum and library, it also has a striking statue of Prithviraj Chauhan on horseback.

Ambitious restoration plans are underway to restore the walls of the first city of Delhi, as also the ancient *baolis* and tombs within the Mehrauli Archaeological Park and Sanjay Van. It would be thrilling to time travel here almost a thousand years into the past to see what ancient Dillika once looked like, and to unravel the mysteries of that time!

Trekking around Dillika

Guess what you might come across if you walked around Dillika, the first city of Delhi? A mysterious iron pillar that never rusts! A victory tower that is the tallest brick minaret in the world, even today! A stepwell said to have magical healing properties! Your adventure will also reveal many ruins, treasures and well-loved legends that have been remembered for almost a thousand years and are sung about to this day!

The Mysterious Iron Pillar of Mehrauli

Delhi's famous Iron Pillar in Mehrauli stands over 7 metres high and weighs over 6 tonnes. Curiously, this pillar has withstood the elements in open air for over 1,600 years without any signs of rusting or corrosion despite being made of 98 per cent wrought iron, which is softer and more ductile than iron. This is indeed a testament to the marvellous expertise achieved by ancient Indian ironsmiths in the extraction and processing of iron. The pillar is said to have resisted corrosion because of its pure composition of iron, a high presence of phosphorous and the unique method of casting. It has intrigued scientists, historians and tourists alike!

The Iron Pillar carries several Sanskrit inscriptions of different dates in the old Brahmi script, suggesting that it was made elsewhere and later carried to Delhi. Who made it and when? Why was it carried to Delhi? The answers all seem to lie in its inscriptions.

Historians have managed to decipher the ancient Sanskrit-Brahmi inscriptions, which provide some clues to the pillar's origins. The oldest one is a six-line description mentioning a king named Chandra. It says that the southern ocean is 'perfumed by the breezes' of Chandra's prowess. This may be a reference to Chandragupta's extension of the Gupta Empire to the Arabian Sea after his conquest of the Western Kshatrapa territory – in present-day Gujarat, Maharashtra, Rajasthan and Madhya Pradesh. So scholars date the making of the pillar to the reign of the Gupta king, Chandragupta II Vikramaditya (375–415 CE).

The Gupta period has been regarded as the Golden Age of India because it was a period of splendid achievements in the arts and sciences. It's likely that this remarkable pillar was made at that time. Scholars also note that the characters of the inscription on the Iron Pillar at Delhi closely resemble the dated inscriptions of Chandragupta II found at the ornately carved Udayagiri caves near Sanchi in Madhya Pradesh, which mention the year 401 CE.

The Iron Pillar inscription describes the king as a devotee of Lord Vishnu and records the erection of a *dhvaja* ('standard' or pillar) of Vishnu on a hill called Vishnupada ('hill of the footprint of Vishnu'). The pillar is considered to be a tribute to Lord Vishnu, the patron deity of the Gupta kings. Scholars also feel that its empty pedestal, which has a deep hole, was once crowned by a figure of Vishnu's carrier, Garuda.

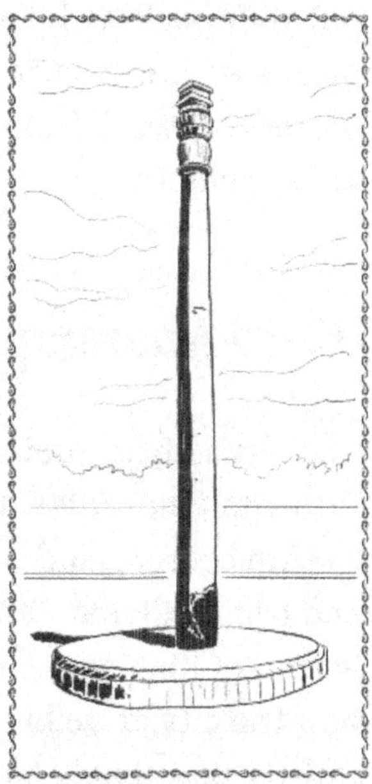

Iron Pillar

Inscription on the Iron Pillar

Another short inscription on the pillar is associated with the Tomar king, Anangapala II, although it is hard to decipher. This has been translated as 'Anangapala tightened the nail (which probably meant the Iron Pillar) in Samvat 1109' (1052 CE).

Using archaeological evidence and facts based on temple architecture, some historians believe that the pillar was brought from its original location in Udayagiri during Tomar times, and erected in the main Tomar temple at the fortress city of Lal Kot. However, all this happened so long ago that one can't be too sure about who built the Iron Pillar or shifted it to Mehrauli. Until definite evidence comes up, this remains one of the unresolved mysteries of Delhi!

This area later became part of the impressive Qutb complex in Mehrauli, where the Iron Pillar still stands, in front of the Quwwat-ul Islam Mosque. It was popularly considered lucky if you could put your back to the pillar and make your hands meet behind to make a wish. However, in 1997, a fence was erected around the iron pillar to protect it from damage. So, it's not possible to try your luck here anymore !

Anangapala and the Iron Pillar

The Rajasthani epic poem, the *Prithvirajaraso* (Songs of Prithviraj), describes the life of King Prithviraj Chauhan in the twelfth century, and is said to have been written by his court poet and friend, Chand Bardai, in 1,300 ballads. It links an interesting legend of King Anangapala II and the Iron Pillar with the story of how the city of Delhi got its name.

It is said that a learned brahmin informed the Rajput ruler that the pillar of solid iron which stood in his territory was so deeply embedded in the earth that its invisible root touched the sacred head of Vasuki, the serpent god. He is believed to balance the burden of the world from the nether regions and ensure that earth remains separate from the netherworld. The brahmin then went on to prophesy that as long as the pillar stood firm and erect, the king and his line of descendants would remain firmly enthroned.

The sceptical king decided to check things out for himself. He ordered the pillar to be pulled out. As the iron shaft was torn out of the earth, its lower end is believed to have emerged dripping with the blood of the immortal serpent king whose head it had pierced. Greatly shaken, Anangapala hastily ordered the Iron Pillar to be immediately re-embedded in the exact same place. This legend may explain the inscription on the Iron Pillar that says: 'Anangapala tightened the nail (or Iron Pillar)...'

However, it is said that the furious and stubborn Vasuki would not let the pillar be replanted firmly again, and despite every effort, it remained shaky and loose, or (in Hindi) '*dhili*'. Folklore goes on to tell us that the city came to be known as 'Dhili' or 'Dilli' since then!

In the next century, when Qutbuddin Aibak took over Delhi, he was said to have heard of the myth surrounding the famous Iron Pillar in his capital city. He was also told of the belief that Hindu rulers would reign over Delhi as long as the Iron Pillar stood there.

However, the disbelieving sultan let the Iron Pillar stand in the courtyard of the mosque in Mehrauli, where, braving the elements for 1,600 years, it stands untarnished to this very day!

Reckless in Love, Fearless in War!

Prithviraj Chauhan is a well-loved hero of Indian folk songs and legends. He is remembered as the audacious king on horseback who boldly carried away the beautiful princess of Kannauj, Samyukta, whom he loved, from the palace of her father, King Jaichand.

The stories of Prithviraj's daring exploits had already swept through the entire country. Samyukta fell in love with him and started corresponding secretly with him in poetry. However, her haughty father, Jaichand, hated Prithviraj with all his heart and would not let her marry him.

As was the custom among royalty in those days, Jaichand held a great *swayamvara* feast at Kannauj, where his daughter would choose her husband from an assembly of great and minor eligible princes, invited from far and near. Of course, Prithviraj did not figure in his list of candidates. On the contrary, a clay statue depicting Prithviraj was placed as a doorkeeper at the gate of venue!

The royal feast began and, attended by her maids, the lovely princess entered, holding a garland of flowers for her chosen one. She walked slowly past the princes present, looking around before placing her garland on the clay statue by the door. As Jaichand and his guests looked on in disbelief, Prithviraj himself appeared on the scene, riding his steed. He swiftly gathered the princess into his arms and lifted her on to his horse before galloping away towards Dillika, his capital, in a cloud of dust.

Unfortunately, they were not destined to live happily ever after. A clash was inevitable between Prithviraj and Muhammad Ghori, whose kingdom now stretched right up to the domains of the Rajput ruler.

After the First Battle of Tarain in 1191 CE, fought between Prithviraj Chauhan and Muhammad Ghori near today's Karnal in Haryana, the latter barely managed to escape with his life. The story goes that he was brought, gravely wounded and in chains, to Prithviraj whom he begged for mercy and release. The chivalrous Rajput released him, much against the wise advice of his ministers. The Afghan invader fled to Afghanistan, vowing to avenge his humiliating defeat at the hands of Prithviraj. This time, he returned with a huge army of about 1,20,000 soldiers.

Spurred on by his brave wife, Prithviraj readied himself to face his old enemy again, believing this to be a mere frontier raid. Also, his father-in-law, King Jaichand of Kannauj, and the ruler of Gujarat – both refused to help him. Jaichand could never forgive Prithviraj for the humiliation he had suffered before an assembly of suitors. Prithviraj also alienated his neighbours by constantly waging war against them, so nobody really came to his aid.

The armies met on the same battlefield as before. This time, the courageous Prithviraj was defeated and killed. It is said that the battlefield of Tarain turned red with blood. As was unfortunately customary for Rajput women at the time, Queen Samyukta and her attendants died by committing *jauhar*, rather than be captured by the enemy.

Sometimes legend takes a different course from history, and is kept alive through folk songs and art. Songs about Prithviraj's bravery are still sung by bards in Rajasthan. The long epic poem, the *Prithvirajaraso*, composed by the court bard, Chand Bardai, narrates several incidents from the life and death of the romantic hero Prithviraj. It tells of how Muhammad Ghori deceitfully defeated him by attacking the Rajput army before daybreak. According to a time-honoured battle code, armies never fought before sunrise or after sunset. The defeated Prithviraj was pursued, caught and taken in chains to Ghor in Afghanistan. As a prisoner in Ghor, he was presented before Muhammad, whom he looked straight in the eye. Muhammad Ghori ordered Prithviraj to lower his eyes, but a defiant Prithviraj scornfully reminded him about the honourable way he had treated Ghori as a prisoner, when the shoe had been on the other foot, reiterating that the eyelids of a Rajput are lowered only in death.

The heroic Prithviraj Chauhan

It is said that Muhammad Ghori flew into a wild rage and ordered that Prithviraj be blinded. He was allegedly brought to the court regularly to be ridiculed by Ghori and his courtiers. Prithviraj was accompanied by his friend, Chand Bardai, who urged Prithviraj to avenge Ghori's betrayal and daily insults.

An opportunity arose when Ghori announced a game of archery. On the advice of Chand Bardai, Prithviraj said he would also like to participate in the contest. Muhammad Ghori and his courtiers guffawed at the blind Rajput. Undaunted, Prithviraj asked Ghori to give the command to shoot, and promised him that he would unerringly hit his target.

Ghori suspiciously asked Prithviraj why he wanted him, and not anyone else, to give the order. Chand Bardai explained to Ghori that, as a king, Prithviraj would not accept orders from anyone other than his equal. Satisfied, Muhammad Ghori agreed.

On the day of the archery contest, Ghori sat in his royal enclosure and had Prithviraj brought to the arena and unchained for the event. His friend, Chand Bardai, muttered to Prithviraj in a couplet:

Dus kadam aagey, bees kadam daein, baitha hai sultan;
Ab mat chuko, Chauhan, chala do apna baan!
(Ten feet ahead of you and 20 feet to your right, is seated the sultan;
Do not miss him now, Chauhan – shoot your arrow!)

When Ghori ordered Prithviraj to shoot, it is said that Prithviraj turned in the direction of Ghori's voice and struck the Afghan dead with his arrow, so unerring was his aim! Chand Bardai and he then shot each other to evade revenge by Ghori's soldiers. And so, the story of Prithviraj Chauhan came to a most tragic end, as was recounted by Chand Bardai's son, who had allegedly witnessed the entire event.

Legends about the times of Prithviraj are included in several medieval epic poems or *kavyas* by Hindu and Jain poets, although they are not really supported by historical evidence. The *Prithvirajraso* that is available to us now was written down many centuries later, with various additions to the original. Muhammad Ghori is actually said to have established a vast empire before he was murdered on his way back to Afghanistan in 1206, fourteen years after the death of Prithviraj Chauhan.

However, the defeat of Prithviraj Chauhan changed the destiny of Delhi forever.

How the Qutb Minar Got Its Name

Controversy surrounds the name of the Qutb Minar, which Qutbuddin Aibak began to construct after completing the Quwwat-ul-Islam Mosque. Was it named after its first builder, or did it get its name from the great Sufi saint and scholar of the time, Khwaja Qutbuddin Bakhtiyar Kaki of the Chishti order? It is said that Aibak named his *minar* after this great *pir*, who was a disciple of Khwaja Moinuddin Chishti. In fact, accounts of the time mention the Qutb Minar as Qutb Sahib Ki Laat after the saint's cane. It was believed to pierce the sky and, like the saint himself, connect heaven and earth.

Qutbuddin Bakhtiyar Kaki is said to have migrated from Baghdad to Delhi and lived here during the reign of the Delhi sultan Iltutmish, who held him in great esteem. He was given the name *Kaki* because of a miracle that he is said to have performed in Delhi.

The story goes that he asked his wife not to take anything on credit from the local baker despite their extreme poverty. Instead, he asked her to pick up *kak* (a kind of bread) from a corner of their house whenever it was needed for the children.

Qutbuddin Bakhtiyar Kaki

And, miraculously, his wife found bread in the corner whenever she required it! The baker, meanwhile, was worried that the Khwaja had stopped taking anything from him because he was annoyed with him. When the baker's wife asked the Khwaja's wife the reason for no longer buying bread from their bakery, the Khwaja's wife told her about the miracle of the *kak*. Although the *kak* stopped appearing after the revelation of the secret, the Sufi saint was called 'Kaki' from then on.

Kaki's shrine is the oldest *dargah* in Delhi. It is close to the Mehrauli Bus Depot and is the venue of the annual *Phoolwalon Ki Sair*. His most famous disciple and spiritual successor was Baba Farid, one of the most revered Sufi saints of Punjab, who, in turn, became the master of Nizamuddin Auliya, Delhi's renowned mystic. Nizamuddin Auliya was himself the teacher of the brilliant Sufi poet and musician, Amir Khusro, as well as Nasiruddin Chirag-e-Dehlavi, his spiritual heir.

It is traditionally believed that Delhi cannot be destroyed as long as the shrine of the revered saint Khwaja Qutbuddin Bakhtiyar Kaki remains here in Mehrauli. Indeed the name 'Mehrauli' is said to come from the Arabic words '*mehr*' and '*wali*' meaning 'blessings' and 'protector' - or blessings of the saint. In fact, Sufi fakirs believe that Kaki is not dead; he has simply drawn a veil around himself so that only the Almighty and the blessed can see him!

Iltutmish Has a Prophetic Dream

The historic city of Delhi stood on parched plains. As its population expanded, the water supply grew inadequate and became an urgent concern for the city.

The Prophet Muhammad himself, mounted on a winged steed, is believed to have appeared to Iltutmish in a dream. In his vision, Buraq, the steed, struck the earth with its hoof, and water gushed out. The Prophet then told the sultan that he should start digging a water tank at the spot where the horse's hoof had struck.

When he woke up in the morning, the sultan rushed to the site of his dream. To his great wonder, he found a hoof print at that very spot where he had seen Buraq paw the ground. Filled with enthusiasm, he began to dig around the hoof print, and water spurted out. He erected a domed pavilion of red sandstone to mark the sacred location. Around it, excavations were made to construct a large water tank. The pavilion rested on twelve pillars within the tank and could be reached only by boat when the tank was full.

This water tank, or reservoir, called Hauz-i-Shamsi (meaning 'sunny water tank'), spread over 20,000 square metres. It would keep the city of Delhi well quenched. Even Ibn Battuta, who came here in 1334, praised its immense size in his writings, saying it stretched approximately two miles in length and one mile in breadth. Its chief water source was rainwater. He also observed: 'When the water level rises high in the tank the dome can be accessed only by boats, but when the water level drops people can walk up to it. Within the dome is a mosque where one always finds fakirs. When the water on the sides of the tank evaporates, sugarcane, cucumber, sweet calabash, melons and watermelons are grown in it.'

The water of this reservoir was considered holy because of its association with the Prophet's wishes and also because of the famous saints and fakirs who visited it later. Nizamuddin is said to have told his disciples that Iltutmish's place in heaven was

Hauz-i-Shamsi – Mehrauli's sunny water tank

assured because he built the Hauz-i-Shamsi for the people of the dry Delhi region. Many famous emperors and saints have been buried on the periphery of this water reservoir.

Today, a park filled with greenery has been laid out around Hauz-i-Shamsi, located at the southern end of Mehrauli. A footbridge connects the pavilion to the park. This area is considered a heritage site today. However, sadly, the water reservoir has almost disappeared beneath the growing layers of garbage.

The Story of Gandhak Ki Baoli

It was the scorching summer of 1230 CE. The heat had made the surrounding areas of Mehrauli unbearably oppressive, and an acute water shortage added to the woes of people living there.

Sultan Iltutmish made an unannounced visit to his spiritual master, the Sufi saint Khwaja Bakhtiyar Kaki, in his *khanqah* in the Mehrauli area. The sultan had always been greatly inspired by the teachings of this great scholar. He was dismayed to find the saint dishevelled and unwashed, and learnt that he had been unable to have regular baths because of the acute water shortage here.

Iltutmish took it upon himself to immediately have a deep stepwell or *baoli* dug near the monastery for the saint and his disciples. It came to be called Gandhak Ki Baoli after the strong sulphur fumes that arose from its water. This smell came from its water source, a sulphur spring, which was said to have curative properties to heal skin diseases.

The simple *baoli* reflected the rainwater harvesting techniques of the time. It was constructed in brick and limestone with five floors that tapered down 105 steps below ground level to a circular water body. There are decorative architectural features with ornate pillared passages on every level. Arcaded verandas with rooms were built on the upper storey for travellers and pilgrims who visited the city and the Sufi monastery. *Baolis* were indeed popular places for social meetings in a cool environment.

Today, the stepwell still fills up with water during the monsoon season. It attracts young divers and swimmers despite its neglected state. It is said that the mossy green water is clear beneath the surface scum. The water is believed to have healing properties even now, and that is why Gandhak Ki Baoli has come to be known as the 'Baoli of Youth'! The secret to its magical curative water lies in its high sulphur content, so a lot of people fill their bottles with this water and take it home for bathing and cleansing.

Razia Sultana: Delhi's Only Queen

The thrilling story of the valiant Razia – the first and last queen of Delhi – is a short and grim one. Razia was nominated by her father, Iltutmish, to succeed him on the throne, for he knew he had no worthwhile heir among his incompetent sons.

However, the nobility hated the very idea of a woman ruler in a male-dominated society. So, after Iltutmish died, Razia's stepbrother, Ruknuddin was crowned sultan of Delhi. Sadly, the new, decadent sultan had little time or inclination for running his kingdom, which he left entirely to Shah Turkaan, his scheming mother. Within six months, rebellions arose from all sides, and both mother and son were put to death.

Meanwhile, Iltutmish's daughter, Razia, appealed to the people of Delhi during Friday prayers, seeking their support as her father's choice. She thus bypassed the nobles and took over the throne with public support.

The nobility now reluctantly accepted Razia, hoping that she would be a puppet in their hands. She was crowned queen of Delhi, and soon proved to be a wise, kind and shrewd ruler. What is more, she was far ahead of her times. Dressed like a man, she refused to wear a veil and led her troops into battle, seated on an elephant. She also mingled freely with her subjects and listened carefully to their grievances. She mastered the art of good governance.

The valiant Razia Sultana

Predictably, her nobles resented her. Their powers were curbed, weakening their hold on the state, as the new queen took independent decisions. Many powerful governors rose in revolt against her. Razia Sultana spent much effort in tackling them, and indeed managed to control the various rebel groups so successfully that she seemed destined to become the most powerful ruler of the Delhi sultanate.

Unfortunately, a chink in Razia's armour led to her undoing. She was rumoured to have a close relationship with an Abyssinian slave called Yakut. Her evident favouritism towards him aroused widespread outrage and resentment among her officers. During a rebellion by Altunia, the governor of Bhatinda, Yakut was killed, and Razia Sultana imprisoned in the Bhatinda Fort. It is believed that Altunia was once a childhood friend and great admirer of Razia. Offended by her relationship with an Abyssinian slave, he rose up in revolt against her. To save her skin and perhaps the throne of Delhi, the hapless queen now agreed to marry Altunia.

However, Razia's woes were far from over. Her stepbrother, Bahram, meanwhile, proclaimed himself sultan of Delhi. Razia and Altunia marched towards Delhi with a big force, but they were defeated by Bahram. Razia's dreams of recapturing Delhi crumbled, and she and Altunia were put to death the very next day. And so, Delhi sadly lost its first and only queen, the valiant Razia. She had ruled Delhi for only four years.

A painting depicting Razia Sultana holding court

Timeline:
1290–1320 CE

3

The Second City
Siri Is Raised

❁ Stories of the Sultanate ❁

The Ilbari sultans were overthrown within less than a century! After them, four celebrated dynasties ruled Delhi before the arrival of the Mughals – the Khiljis, the Tughlaks, the Sayyids and the Lodis. Each came to Delhi spurred by a single-minded ambition to build the empire of their dreams here.

Like the Ilbari Turks, the Khiljis were descendants of the Turks, but had been long settled in Afghanistan in a village called Khalj from which they got their name. Jalaluddin Khilji overthrew Balban's successors to found the Khilji dynasty, which controlled large parts of northern India for about thirty years.

Said to be generous and generally mild, he was about seventy years old when he ascended the throne of the Delhi sultanate.

Jalaluddin Khilji

However, fearing the hostility of the nobles and the people of Delhi after he murdered young Kaikobad, the grandson and successor of Balban, Jalaluddin Khilji chose to rule from the suburb of Killu Ghari or Kilokri. Sultan Kaikobad had laid the foundations of a large palace and garden here in Kilokri, on the banks of the River Yamuna, and it developed into a bustling town. Jalaluddin now ordered the completion of the palace along with the construction of a fort and watchtower. This is where he preferred to stay. However, he was sultan for only six years.

His reign was cut short by the ruthless and determined Alauddin Khilji, who killed Jalaluddin, who was his uncle and father-in-law. It is said that Alauddin entered the capital city in pouring rain with his uncle's head on a pike and proclaimed himself the new sultan. Following many fierce conquests of Hindu kingdoms - Gujarat, Ranthambore, Chittor, Malwa, Siwana and Jalore - he soon controlled almost all of the north, and extended the boundaries of the Delhi sultanate beyond the Vindhyas to the Deccan in Devagiri, Warangal, Dwarasamudra, and Madura.

The city of Siri, which he constructed, served as the seat of Alauddin's power during his frequent campaigns to expand his territory. The conquest of Chittor was the biggest success in the history of the Khilji dynasty. Many modern historians question the authenticity of the famous legend of the brave and beautiful Rani Padmini of Chittor and the infatuated Alauddin Khilji, who was determined to take her away, although his siege of Chittor in 1303 CE is a historical event. Over the centuries, Rani Padmini came to be seen as a tragic figure, and even today, folk songs are sung in memory of the queen and her ladies-in-waiting who, sadly, committed *jauhar*.

Rani Padmini of Chittor

The imperial city of Delhi was constantly threatened by wave upon wave of ferocious Mongol tribesmen from Central Asia. They had been descending in hordes to plunder the northern kingdoms ever since the thirteenth century. During Alauddin's reign, a multitude of Mongols invaded the north, penetrating it as far as Delhi,

An unusual portrait of the warlike Alauddin Khilji

and looting the defenceless outskirts. Alauddin entrenched his army in Siri, which lay about 5 kilometres north-east of the Qutb Minar, and managed to drive back the fierce fighters.

Alauddin Khilji constructed Siri, the second city of Delhi, on this flat battlefield, around 1303 CE, to defend his empire from any further Mongol invasions. It was built as a strong fortress of stone and brick, resembling the massive Turkish forts, against the marauding Mongols. Indeed, Alauddin's strong repulsion of the Mongols was a major achievement in safeguarding the destiny of Delhi from Mongol rule.

The frequent Mongol invasions in West Asia had driven some of the Seljuqs of the great Seljuq Empire, which had once stretched from modern-day Iran to Turkey, to seek asylum in Delhi. The craftsmen of this dynasty brought with them their rich architectural traditions and skills. These were very distinctive, using stone and brick with elaborate geometric and calligraphic decoration. Their towering minarets often had square or octagonal shapes. The Seljuqs are credited with many of the architectural marvels of this era built in Siri.

We know from the memoirs of Timur that Alauddin's 'round city' was built on a large scale with palaces and other edifices. It had seven gates for people to enter or exit. According to the famous Moroccan scholar and globetrotter, Ibn Battuta, its walls were 17 feet thick. The main palace of the fort, 'Hazaar Sutun' (or the beautiful marble 'Palace of a Thousand Pillars') stood inside, lavishly decorated and inlaid with precious stones. This was the pride of the new city of Siri.

Alauddin Khilji was indeed a prolific builder. He also built the famous Alai Darwaza, a magnificent ceremonial gateway that welcomes visitors to the Qutb complex. Complete with inlaid marble work and latticed stone screens, it represented a new style of architecture at the time, the Indo-Islamic style. It is considered the first structure in India with a dome built on scientific lines, featuring pointed rather than round arches. Red sandstone surfaces with marble inlay work and windows fitted with perforated screens characterized this new style of architecture. There was intricate decoration everywhere, with interlaced flowing lines and inspirational texts.

He built a *madrasa* close to the *minar*. What is more, he also dreamt of building a *minar* twice as high and wide as the Qutb and began construction in real earnest. However, the Alai Minar had reached only one storey when he died. It remained unfinished and stands to this day in the shadow of the Qutb Minar.

Alauddin dug a vast reservoir at Hauz-i-Alai or Hauz Khas, meaning 'special water tank' for the city of Siri. Little remains

The magnificent Alai Darwaza

The unfinished Alai Minar

of Siri today, but the Hauz Khas reservoir still stands, although it fell into disuse soon after his death.

A stern but efficient administrator, Alauddin undertook several large-scale reforms to centralize power in his hands. Indeed, his reign was known for its harsh measures and punishments. He introduced revenue and land reforms, and he was the first sultan to use an assessment based on measurement and yield per area unit of arable land. Large markets came up and the prices of essential goods were effectively controlled for his soldiers as well as for the common man. In fact, it is said, he kept all prices unchanged for twenty years!

The Mongol invasions as also many internal uprisings had necessitated the maintenance of a large standing army. It was disciplined and well organized. Horses were branded and soldiers given identity documents. The suspicious sultan set up an efficient spy system and everyone was under close surveillance. It was said then that even the walls had eyes and ears! Alcohol and gambling were strictly forbidden as were secret gatherings or parties among nobles and officers.

Alauddin's many military campaigns enabled him to amass much wealth. He had coins minted in silver and gold using the grand title of 'Sikander Sani' or Alexander the Second, in recognition of his military prowess. This title is also inscribed on the Alai Darwaza. Indeed, he had a grandiose image of himself, firmly believing in the divine right of the ruler. Therefore, unlike all the previous rulers of Delhi, he never felt the need to consult the Muslim clergy on matters of state. According to the fourteenth-century scholar and historian, Barani, he was the first sultan to separate religion from the state.

Although he could barely read or write himself, Alauddin Khilji encouraged the arts. The famous poet Amir Khusro, often considered the father of north Indian classical music, was a prominent figure in his court.

These were good times for the Delhi sultanate. Delhi flourished as the imperial capital of the largest and most powerful empire of northern India, surviving factional disputes, stiff resistance from the Rajputs and external threats from the Mongols. Ibn Battuta, whose extensive travels covered some 1,20,700 kilometres as far as China and Sumatra, was impressed enough to describe fourteenth-century Delhi as 'one of the greatest cities of the universe'. Alauddin was indisputably the most significant sultan of the Khilji dynasty with his long reign of two decades.

However, Alauddin's dream of a vast and stable empire began to fade with the breaking away of several territories even before his death. Indeed, the next four years after him saw sultans in Delhi come and go in quick succession.

The ruins of Killu Ghari, or today's Kilokri, did not withstand the ravages of time. This congested urban village, once an imperial capital, lies between Maharani Bagh and Jangpura in south-east Delhi, with no remnants of the lost medieval city.

Today, the site of the historic Siri Fort lies in the heart of Delhi, between Green Park and Hauz Khas metro stations. The city of Siri is currently occupied by the village of Shahpur Jat, Sheikh Sarai, Hauz Khas, Green Park and Panchsheel Enclave, but hardly any of its famed walls remain. The destruction of the Fort is attributed to several successive rulers who removed its stones, bricks and other building materials for their own buildings. Some walls are said to have been removed by the Afghan ruler Sher Shah well over 200 years later, to build the walls of his city – the sixth city of Delhi. However, certain parts – up to 3 kilometres long, still lie buried. Future excavations may reveal these historical parts of the fourteenth century Siri Fort

The ruins of Siri Fort

wall. Archaeologists also hope to find skeletal remains of Mongol soldiers buried inside the fortification walls and rediscover the history of the site.

Siri Fort Auditorium is today a premier multi-auditorium complex of the Indian government. A prestigious entertainment centre in New Delhi, film festivals, dance performances, plays and music recitals are regularly organized here. Close by stands the Asiad Games Village Complex, popularly known as the Siri Fort Sports Complex, which has been developed around the ruins. Situated in the heart of south Delhi, it is well equipped with world-class sports facilities.

The Archaeological Survey of India (ASI), the custodian of heritage monuments in Delhi, has begun restoration work on several ancient structures, which include the walls of the Siri Fort. Recent excavations here have also led to the unexpected discovery of a hidden underground tunnel of the period, raising many exciting questions. Does the tunnel lead to a secret chamber? Hidden treasure? Mongol heads? Or a concealed passageway to evade enemies? Perhaps the mysteries of Siri Fort will be solved as soon as the excavators complete their work. Until then, we can only wait and watch!

Gold coins from the reign of Alauddin Khilji

Tales around Siri

Diverse tales of violence, literary genius and valour pervade the second city of Siri and those linked to it.

The Lost City of Kilokri

Killu Ghari or Kilokri was once a quiet plain on the banks of the River Yamuna, about 16 kilometres east of Mehrauli. Khwaja Bakhtiyar Kaki had first settled here after he left Multan, which was then under siege by the Mongols. The proximity of this tranquil place to the River Yamuna was very appealing and he set up his monastery here. However, Sultan Iltutmish, his nobles and theologians had to travel a considerable distance from the capital city to meet the great Sufi saint here. Much against his wishes, the Khwaja was persuaded to move to Mehrauli, where he spent the rest of his life.

The peaceful Sufi settlement of Kilokri later turned into a hotbed of politics where plots were hatched against the successors of Iltutmish. Ruknuddin, one of Raziya's stepbrothers, marched here with his forces to put down rebels but ended up being executed himself.

It was the grandson and successor of Balban, the teenage sultan, Kaikobad, who is credited with the founding of a new city here. According to Barani, he was 'a handsome young man of excellent qualities with a heart filled with the desire to enjoy the pleasures of life'. He laid the foundations of a grand palace of mirrors and garden on the banks of the River Yamuna. The new city, or *sher-i-nau*, abounded with singers, dancers and court jesters. The overpopulated Qutb Dilli came to be called the 'old' city. Festivals like Nauroz, the Persian New Year, were celebrated with great enthusiasm - in fact, a long poem by Amir Khusro describes these revelries in Kilokri. The nobility started constructing their palaces here, and with the migration of merchants and civilians to Kilokri, it became a beautiful and thriving city.

The killing of Kaikobad in his own palace by Jalaluddin Khilji marked the beginning of the Khilji dynasty, bringing him to the throne of the Delhi sultanate. The new sultan preferred to reside in Kilokri, fearing the hostility of the residents of the capital city. A new round of construction saw the expansion of the grand palace and gardens, along with a stone fort and watchtowers. As more people flocked to the new city, busy markets sprang up here, as also a new mosque.

North of Kilokri, barely 2 kilometres away, lay Ghiyaspur, where Nizamuddin Auliya was constructing his monastery. It is said that he would walk down to Kilokri for the Friday prayers, increasingly unhappy about the bustling traffic on his way.

More blood was spilled as Alauddin Khilji seized the throne from his uncle to crown himself sultan of Delhi. Kilokri faded into oblivion. Today, it's an unplanned urban village between Maharani Bagh and Jangpura. No evidence remains of Kaikobad's grand palace or gardens here. Sadly, hardly anyone even knows that this once-imperial city ever existed!

The Wall of Heads: Siri Fort

Siri Fort stands in the heart of the city, and a gory story lies behind this name.

Those were harsh times indeed. Although a series of Mongol marauders besieged Siri Fort, they could not penetrate its walls and were compelled to retreat six times. Alauddin chased them out aggressively and finally drove them north of Kabul in 1306. This ensured that the Mongols would not attack the frontier kingdoms again for some time. He reinforced his border defences to keep the Mongols away during all their subsequent attacks.

'Siri' derives its name from '*sir*' or head in Hindi. According to the many stories of Alauddin's war exploits, the foundations of this mighty fort were built on 8,000 severed heads of Mongol soldiers killed by his army!

Another story tells us about the routing of the Mongol army by Alauddin after their plunder of Punjab and Amroha. Thousands of captured soldiers were allegedly brought to Siri and ruthlessly trampled upon by elephants. Their severed heads were then said to have been hung from the walls of Siri Fort. Pyramids of heads were also said to have been assembled here. These were probably designed to serve as a dire warning to the Mongols that this would be their fate if they dared to invade ever again!

Alauddin's deterrent punishments were unstoppable. He also built the Chor Minar or 'Tower of Thieves' outside the walls of Siri. It has a gruesome history according to local legend for it was, in reality, a 'tower of decapitation'. Here the severed heads of thieves and other criminals were impaled on long spears and displayed through the 225 holes of the tower. This seems to have been a common practice in medieval times where openings in the walls of the towers were not merely used as windows! And if the beheaded number of heads exceeded the number of holes, the heads of lesser criminals were simply piled in a pyramid outside the Chor Minar for display!

The Chor Minar stands in the posh Hauz Khas area today, just off Aurobindo Marg and opposite the market. The lush greenery around it serves as a park, beautifully laid out and in blissful

Chor Minar

ignorance of its sordid history. The *minar* is kept locked and, not surprisingly, is said to be haunted at night!

The 'Delhi Decapitator' as Alauddin has come to be morbidly nicknamed in popular culture today, featuring as he does in several plays, television serials and films, thus managed to rule for twenty long years with a brutal hand, even during those very turbulent times!

Mystic and Musician: Amir Khusro

Let me ask a riddle,
Listen, O my son,
She flew without wings,
With a thread in her neck.[1]

All twenty lost their heads.
No life was lost, no blood was shed.[2]

She flares up when the wind blows,
And drinks water only to die.
A flaming beauty is she –
Yet she's not a woman – just 'she'.[3]

Playful and enigmatic, these riddles were authored by the gifted Amir Khusro, a Sufi mystic of Turkish origin, who was a nobleman in the court of Alauddin Khilji. A multi-talented man, this poet and musician had a brilliant career spanning fifty years in the royal courts of more than seven kings of the Delhi sultanate!

Amir Khusro studied under the revered Sufi saint, Nizamuddin Auliya of Delhi, with whom he eventually settled down. His prolific and unique poetry won him admiration and recognition in the court. He kept the company of sultans, intellectuals and Sufi mystics, and became one of India's greatest poets, composing lyrics, odes, epics and elegies. Khusro also wrote riddles and sayings, which the common masses enjoyed.

Amir Khusro indeed represents the beginning of Indian-based Persian and Islamic literature, which evolved into a unique syncretic culture, with Indian imagery and sentiment. He played an important role in the development of 'Hindavi', a dialect of

1. A kite; 2. Toenails and fingernails; 3. Fire

Amir Khusro (centre) with his disciples

Braj Bhasha that was spoken around Delhi, and which would evolve into the Hindustani language. What is more, he was also the founder of both Hindustani classical music and the style of singing called *qawwali* – the devotional music of the Sufis. It is popularly believed that the sitar and tabla are his inventions too!

However, the pleasures of court life did not diminish the teachings of his spiritual master, Hazrat Nizamuddin Auliya, with whom he shared a close bond. Even today, on Basant Panchami, a concert is organized every year in his memory at his tomb in Nizamuddin, where he lies buried at the feet of his master.

Born and raised in Hindustan, Amir Khusro was a true son of the soil. He identified himself as a 'Turk-i-Hindustani' – a Hindustani Turk, styling himself as 'Tuti-i-Hind' or the 'Parrot of Hindustan'.

Here, renowned musicians perform his inimitable compositions, dedicated to spring:

> *Rejoice, my love, rejoice,*
> *It's spring here, rejoice!*

A charming story lies behind these celebrations. It is said that the Sufi saint was upset over the loss of his dear nephew, and had stopped smiling. On his way to visit him from Mehrauli, Amir

An illustrated page of one of Amir Khusro's poems

Khusro passed a group of farm labourers wearing yellow scarves round their necks, and happily carrying bright mustard flowers. They were on their way to the local temple to offer gratitude for a good spring harvest. Khusro borrowed a scarf, and tying it round his head, walked all the way to his master, singing couplets on spring that he created on the way. 'I'm doing all this to make you smile,' he told the saint. And, indeed, Nizamuddin Auliya did smile, after six months!

Ever since that time, almost 700 years ago, the Basant Panchami celebrations at the shrine have become an annual tradition. All lanes leading here are carpeted with yellow flowers, mostly marigolds, drawing thousands of visitors of all faiths, draped in yellow scarves and turbans. The graves of both Nizamuddin and Amir Khusro are offered yellow *chaadar*s, and Khusro's qawwalis welcoming spring are sung in the evening. It's indeed a unique celebration of a Hindu festival in a mosque!

In fact, Amir Khusro's literary gems and compositions can be heard in *qawwalis* at music festivals and Sufi *dargahs* across South Asia, even seven centuries after his death. That is why he is called immortal!

Look at this classic Farsi couplet he wrote about the stunning Kashmir valley:

If there be heaven on earth,
It is this, it is this, it is this.

What is more, his words overflowed with love for Delhi as well. He wrote:

Delhi is my country, my city, the most beautiful city in the world.

He is indeed one of the most celebrated Delhiwallahs of all time!

Timeline:
1320–25 CE

4

The Third City Tughlakabad Is Built

Tales of the Tughlaks

Those were eventful times indeed! Many a sultan came and went in the ancient capital city of Delhi, each changing its face with enduring structures and enriching its culture. It was with the coming of the Tughlaks that the third city of Delhi was raised.

The new city was appropriately called Tughlakabad after its founder, Ghazi Malik, better known as Ghiyasuddin Tughlak. A Turkish governor, he was a seasoned old campaigner of Alauddin Khilji's army. He marched to Delhi and wrested the throne from Khusro Khan, who had killed the last of the Khiljis, thus putting an end to the turbulent period following Alauddin's death. However, his reign as sultan was a short one, lasting barely five years.

Ghiyasuddin Tughlak

When Ghiyasuddin ascended the throne in 1320 CE, he was a crusty old warrior, accustomed to facing the constant onslaught of enemies in the frontier provinces. This was, moreover, a period of political unrest, with the perpetual danger of Mongol attacks from the north-western borders of the empire.

The new sultan dreamt of an invincible capital city, which

would keep all Mongol marauders at bay and where its denizens could feel protected. He found the low walls of the existing capital of Siri most inadequate and insecure. He decided to move south-east towards a rocky hill of the Aravalli range and build a new city around it. This would give him the natural fortification and defensible location that he sought.

A great fort was raised 8 kilometres away from the Qutb Minar, as protection against all possible Mongol raids. Its magnificent ramparts, battlements and mammoth stonework displayed the architectural skills of its craftsmen. Its walls were 10 to 15 metres high. The fort city had as many as fifty-two gates to lead through these massive walls. And so the imposing city of Tughlakabad, a symbol of royal strength, was born.

However, Ghiyasuddin's grand plans came to nought very soon. The rocky terrain was too dry and the site had to be soon abandoned because of severe water shortages. So, once again, the capital returned to its old site near the Qutb Minar.

Today, most of the dream city of Tughlakabad is inaccessible due to its dense thorny vegetation. The splendid fort and tomb

Ruins of Tughlakabad Fort

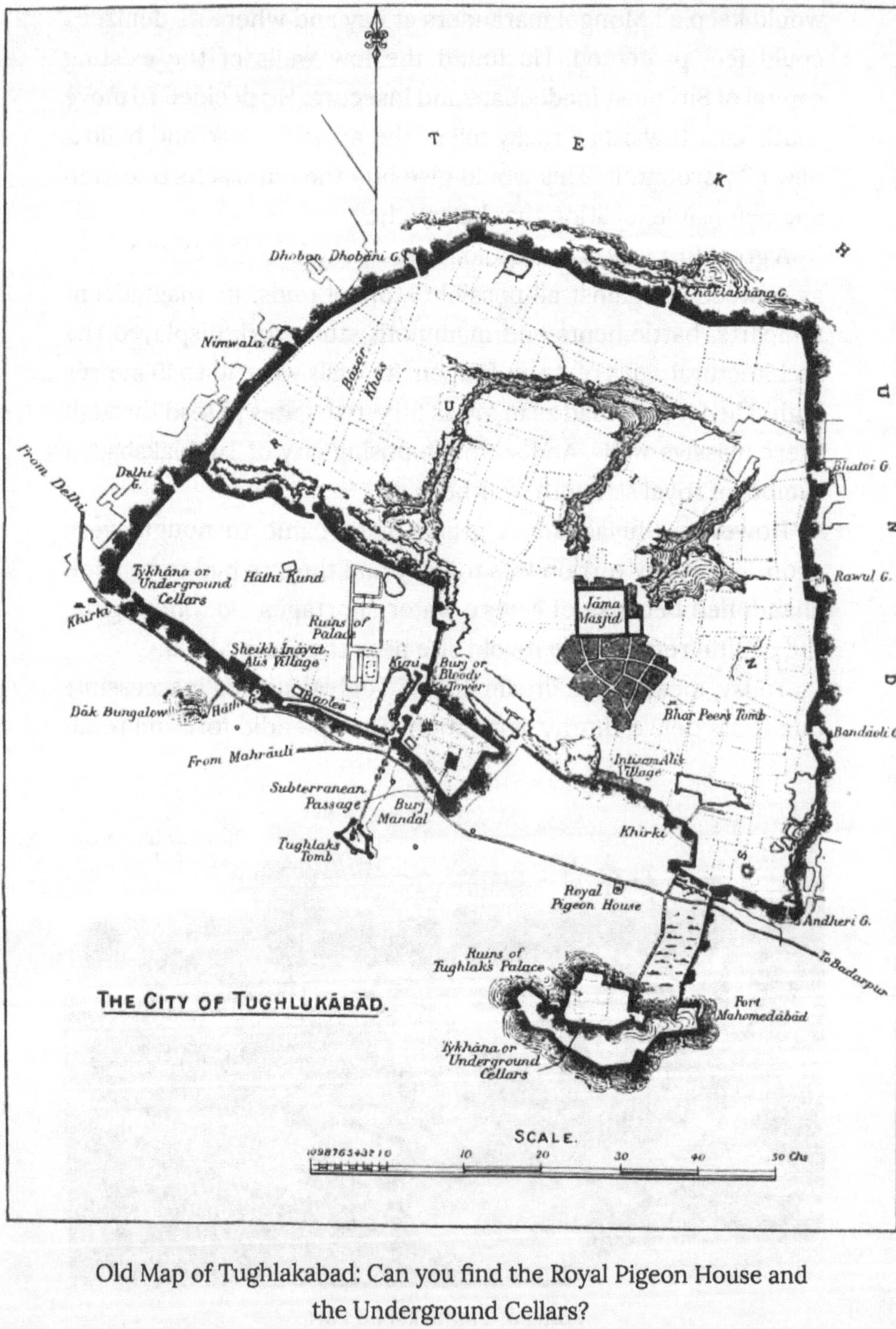

Old Map of Tughlakabad: Can you find the Royal Pigeon House and the Underground Cellars?

that houses three graves - those of Ghiyasuddin, his wife and his son and successor, Muhammad bin Tughlak - still stand today on the rocky terrain, although in ruins. Only thirteen of the fort's magnificent gates remain. This third city of Delhi lies completely deserted on the south-eastern edge of New Delhi, off the Mehrauli-Badarpur Road.

However, modern settlements, rough shanties and a commercial area have come up below the fort. The Tughlakabad Institutional Area stands in the vicinity. The Inland Container Depot (ICD), India's largest dry port, is situated here and handles nearly 2000 containers a day for north India. A 'dry' port is an inland container depot that handles and stores containers, and is well connected to a seaport and the rest of the country by road or rail.

The Dr Karni Singh Shooting Range and Okhla Industrial Area also stand close by.

A tunnel in Tughlakabad

Legends of Tughlakabad

The sultans and Sufi saints sometimes shared a hostile relationship. The rocky capital city of Tughlakabad resonates with many astounding legends.

The Curse of the Saint

It is traditionally believed that the real reason for the desertion of Tughlakabad was a curse against the place by the great mystic of the time, Hazrat Nizamuddin Auliya. 'Auliya' means Friend of God, and people always flocked to him for his blessings.

Throughout his reign, Ghiyasuddin Tughlak remained hostile and resentful of the Sufi saint's great popularity with the people of Delhi, and tried, whenever he could, to diminish his hold over them.

This was not really unusual because, at that time, the relationship between the Sufis and the state was often strained. Several sultans were wary of the growing popularity of Sufis, fearing their influence could erode royal authority. Hazrat Nizamuddin's disciples would address him with awe-inspiring titles like Sultan ul-Mashaikh (sultan of the sheikhs), raising him to a status as exalted as the sultan's. So the suspicious Ghiyasuddin believed that the Sufi saint and his disciples were trying to usurp his power. What was more, much to his resentment, even his

Nizamuddin Auliya

son and heir, Prince Jauna, the future Muhammad bin Tughlak, was deeply devoted to the saint.

When the sultan was building his great fort at Tughlakabad, he wanted every mason available for this massive task. Hazrat Nizamuddin Auliya was, at that same time, busy building his *baoli* or stepwell in his small village of Ghiyaspur, about 12 kilometres away. This village lay on the outskirts of Delhi but was a part of the sultan's empire.

The sultan imperiously forbade any of the masons to work for the Auliya. The sympathetic masons, however, offered to help the saint by working for him at night, by the light of oil lamps. When the hot-headed Ghiyasuddin came to know of this, he stopped the supply of all oil to the saint. It is said that the workers continued to light their lamps miraculously with water from the *baoli* and completed their work of construction.

Annoyed with the sultan's constant malice, Hazrat Nizamuddin Auliya cursed the new city of Tughlakabad: 'May it remain barren or be only a habitation for shepherds!'

Once a symbol of the might of the Tughlak Empire, the rocky and arid capital city of Tughlakabad was abandoned within five years. For a long time thereafter, it was frequented only by shepherds and nomads. Indeed, eternal desolation has resonated here through history – right down to this day!

'Delhi is Still Far Away'

Obstinate and arrogant, Ghiyasuddin Tughlak remained at loggerheads with the Sufi saint Hazrat Nizamuddin Auliya all his life.

After the sultan's triumph in Bengal in 1324 CE, where he took advantage of a civil war to annex its territory, he planned a victorious return to Tughlakabad, his kingdom's capital. He ordered his son, Prince Jauna, to construct a wooden pavilion for a grand celebration of the father-and-son reunion in Tughlakabad. However, before this visit, Ghiyasuddin petulantly ordered the Sufi mystic to clear out of Ghiyaspur where he lived.

During the span of these years, Ghiyaspur had grown from a small settlement into a major pilgrimage centre. People came here from far and wide, drawn by the austerity and fame of the Sufi saint as also his beloved disciple, the famous mystic poet, Amir Khusro.

Sultan Ghiyasuddin was, in fact, very fond of Amir Khusro, who was also his court poet. When the sultan decreed that Hazrat Nizamuddin Auliya should leave Delhi immediately before his return, Amir Khusro, who revered the Sufi saint deeply, came to the sultan and voiced his concern about the peremptory order. However, the mystic saint himself was not unduly perturbed by the sultan's persistent rancour. Instead, he uttered his famous Farsi phrase: '*Hanooz Dilli dur ast* (Delhi is still far away).' Then, a strange thing happened. It is said that, following the arrival of the sultan at the Afghanpur Pavilion in Tughlakabad, constructed by his son, the weather abruptly turned stormy. A bolt of lightning struck the wooden structure, and the sultan was electrocuted on the spot.

Another story goes that Muhammad bin Tughlak ordered that several elephants be made to stomp in the vicinity of the pavilion, causing the whole structure to vibrate and collapse on the sultan, crushing him to death. It is quite likely that Muhammad bin Tughlak had hatched this deadly plot to gain the throne. Nevertheless, the Auliya's barb had come true!

Many centuries later, Tughlakabad lies in desolate ruins today. The *dargah* of Hazrat Nizamuddin Auliya, in central Delhi's Nizamuddin West area, is a venerated destination.

'Beloved of God' – Hazrat Nizamuddin Auliya

'Be like a large tree so that Allah's creation, the vast multitude of human beings, may find rest and solace beneath your shadow.'

Saying this, Khwaja Fariduddin Ganjshakar, better known as Baba Farid, removed the turban that he had received from his own Sufi master, Khwaja Bakhtiyar Kaki, and placed it on the head of young Nizamuddin who knelt before him to seek his blessings.

Baba Farid

'My son, the spark has been lit,' he said. 'You have completed your task and pleased Allah. I now give the *wilayat* (guardianship) of Hindustan to you. Devote yourself single-mindedly to this great mission...' Summoning all his disciples, he announced, 'Today I give the *taj* (crown) of the Sufis to Nizamuddin. May Allah help him always.'

It was the highest honour! The young Shaikh bowed his head in humility and wept.

Every year, Shaikh Nizamuddin would travel from Delhi, where he lived, all the way to Ajodhan (now Pakpattan Sharif in Pakistan) to be with his master during the holy month of Ramadan. Baba Farid had initiated him into the well-known Chishti order of the Sufis, giving him the most intense spiritual training. As soon as he was in Ajodhan, Nizamuddin would serve him with utmost devotion, and spend much of his time in chanting, prayer and meditation. He would then return home to practise all that he had learnt. With time, he had mastered the teachings of the Sufi tradition, and the way to self-purification and spiritual perfection.

Nizamuddin visited his master three times. This would be his last visit, Baba Farid knew. When he reached Delhi, Nizamuddin received the news of his master's death.

Hazrat Nizamuddin Auliya of Delhi was now the new master of the Chishti Sufi order! People of all faiths thronged to meet him and seek his blessings. He welcomed many new disciples into the order, and sent them far and wide to spread the word of Allah.

After a while, he longed for solitude. He was inspired by a divine voice to move away from the noisy vicinity of the Qutb Minar where he lived, to Ghiyaspur, a quiet settlement on the outskirts of Delhi, around 1266 CE. Here, by the banks of the River Yamuna, he built a rough shed with a straw roof for himself and his followers. They lived simply, often in great hardship, with hardly anything to eat, their souls nourished simply by prayer and meditation! It was not long before his *khanqah* began to throng with people from all walks of life. Much later, in 1321 CE, he began construction of his *baoli* here. It is said that he began work on the stepwell by digging the earth with his own hands while declaring, 'He who drinks one drop of its water should have no fear of the fires of Hell.'

Hazrat Nizamuddin Auliya lived in Ghiyaspur for almost sixty years, during which time the throne of Delhi saw seven monarchs come and go. Yet, he would have nothing to do with sultans or their courts. One day, Sultan Jalaluddin Khilji wanted to pay a visit to Hazrat Nizamuddin's *khanqah.* The master refused, sending a terse message, 'My house has two doors. If the sultan enters through one, I will exit through the other.'

Popularly known as '*Mehboob-i-Illahi*' or 'beloved of God', this great Sufi saint was known for his great wisdom, compassion and generosity. He had known what it was like to go hungry in his early days at Ghiyaspur, and so he distributed food every day to thousands of needy people at his spiritual centre, without any social or religious discrimination, right up to the time of his death in 1325 CE, at the age of eighty-seven.

Dargah of Nizamuddin Auliya

The village of Ghiyaspur came to be renamed 'Nizamuddin' after the revered saint, and people converged here for his blessing.

After his death, Hazrat Nizamuddin Auliya's *dargah*, his final resting place across the road, became one of the most venerated shrines in Delhi. The *baoli* is still in use, fed by an underwater spring, and its waters are considered sacred. Many later monarchs wished to be buried near his grave as well. Humayun's Tomb borders Nizamuddin's shrine. Princess Jahanara, beloved daughter of Shah Jahan, is buried within the *dargah* in an open-air chamber, as is the lesser-known later Mughal king, Muhammad Shah 'Rangila', in an adjoining enclosure. The Sufi saint also left behind several well-known disciples, including his successor, Nasiruddin Chiragh-e-Dehlavi, and the acclaimed mystic poet Amir Khusro, who is buried at his feet.

The elegant residential area of Nizamuddin in central Delhi, just off Mathura Road, is a popular tourist and pilgrimage destination today. Across the road from the majestic Humayun's Tomb, people of all religions from far and wide gather to see the shrine and *baoli* of the revered mystic, Hazrat Nizamuddin Auliya. Devotional songs or *qawwali* were an important feature in the lives of the Sufi mystics and, to this day, *qawwali* singers perform here after the evening prayers, filling the air with music and song. A favourite *qawwali* sung here is Amir Khusro's '*Dama Dam Mast Qalandar*', *in* praise of the revered Sufi saint Shahbaaz Qalandar:

Oh, the red-robed one, please protect me always, Jhulelaal –
The friend of Sindh and Sehwan, Shahbaaz Qalandar,
My breath is for the God-intoxicated saint,
Glory be to you!

However, several historical structures that once came up around the wall of the great Sufi saint's *baoli*, have sadly got lost in the densely populated Nizamuddin Basti today, in a maze of rampant unauthorized encroachments and construction.

Timeline:
1325–51 CE

5

The Fourth City Jahanpanah, Refuge of the World

❁ Tales of Tumultuous Times ❁

The Tughlaks were, indeed, a remarkable dynasty of builders: three different Tughlak kings built a city each in Delhi – Tughlakabad, Jahanpanah and Firozabad.

A fascinating but rather eccentric character, Muhammad bin Tughlak took over the reins of the empire after his father's sudden death in 1325 CE. He was perhaps the most controversial of all the sultans of Delhi – and was even called crazy. Yet he was intelligent and, in some matters, often well ahead of his times.

He abandoned Tughlakabad within five years because of its water shortages. And so, the capital shifted once again to its old site near the Qutb Minar.

The insecurity of the large population that resided in the open plains between Dilli and Siri prompted Muhammad bin Tughlak to start building new fortifications against any possible Mongol attacks. He attempted to combine the three previous cities of Delhi – Dilli, Siri and Tughlakabad – and called this enclosure Jahanpanah or the Refuge of the World. This was his new capital; thus Delhi's fourth city, Jahanpanah, came into being. However, the sultan realized that the cost of building fortifications would be exorbitant and eventually gave up that idea.

Historians believe that the fortified city contained the palace complex and the main mosque for the sultan and the royal household, while the majority of the city's population continued to live within the walls of the Lal Kot Fort in Dilli.

Bijay Mandal Fort

Within Jahanpanah, Muhammad bin Tughlak made major additions to the Bijay Mandal Fort, believed to have been built earlier by Alauddin Khilji. The sultan embellished Bijay Mandal Fort by constructing a grand 'Hall of a Thousand Pillars' called 'Hazaar Sutun', which served as a vast hall for public audience. Its pillars were made of carved wood and supported an exquisitely carved wooden roof.

It was here that the Moroccan traveller, Ibn Battuta, is said to have met Muhammad bin Tughlaq after he arrived in Delhi in 1333 CE. The scholar visited the court of the sultan and stayed on here for nearly eight years. Battuta's account of his time under the sultan's patronage provides a glimpse of the grandeur of Bijay Mandal, where ornamented elephants guarded the three entrances of the palace. He also tells us of the sultan's private chambers, and a central octagonal watchtower from where the sultan could monitor his troops and the entire city too.

However, even Jahanpanah was not destined to remain the capital city for long. Convinced that it lay too far north to be an effective capital for his extensive empire, Muhammad bin Tughlak made the fort city of Devagiri in the Deccan his new capital city and administrative centre, renaming it Daulatabad or 'Abode of Wealth'. This would help maintain more control over the south, he reasoned, as also safeguard his capital from Mongol attacks in the north. However, instead of moving just the royal offices, it is said that he forcibly uprooted and moved most of Jahanpanah's inhabitants over a thousand kilometres south to Daulatabad. He is believed to have made this far-reaching decision without consulting his nobles.

He single-handedly caused a decline in the fortunes of the city of Jahanpanah! Thousands perished during the exhausting journey of over 1,500 kilometres despite the facilities provided along the way. Worse, the plan proved disastrous because of an acute water scarcity in Daulatabad. The sultan also realized that his new capital was too far away to protect the north from the threat of Mongol attacks. Eight years later, he abandoned Daulatabad in favour of the more central city of Jahanpanah. And the move back began all over again!

The experiment proved a costly one, leading to great discontent and depopulating the city considerably. The sultan tried his best to make amends, and invited many scholars and artists to settle in the city. A severe famine a few years later only added to the many miseries of its people.

It was said that Delhi remained like a ghost city for years afterwards. 'When I entered Delhi, it was almost like a desert,' wrote Ibn Battuta, who had once been in raptures over the splendour of the city.

Today, although the remains of the city of Jahanpanah are mostly well hidden in the village of Khirki, beyond present-day Press Enclave, some of its walls are still visible behind the Indian Institute of Technology and the Begumpuri Masjid. The Bijay Mandal Palace has been reduced to neglected ruins amid shrubs, scattered rubble and garbage dumps behind today's Sarvapriya Vihar. The walls and pillars have crumbled and only deep sockets in the ground, where the wooden pillars were once fixed, remain. You can also see holes in the ground within the chambers, which may have been used for burying treasure.

However, its watchtower still gives a spectacular view of the city, from the Qutb Minar to the Lotus Temple, just as it must have given the sultan, always on the lookout for enemies, in the fourteenth century!

The rest of the capital city of Jahanpanah has practically disappeared under thick forest cover today. It extends over 400 acres between Tughlakabad and Chirag Dilli. Jahanpanah City Forest is South Delhi's largest green lung, with a 7-kilometre jogging track – indeed, the longest in a city forest. Morning walkers, joggers and nature enthusiasts frequent the dense forest where the air is heavy with fragrances. Deeper in the forest, the intense silence is broken only by the call of birds and the occasional peacock cry. One could well lose track of time here. Nevertheless, the gleam of dish antennae over the overgrown *keekar* treetops brings one firmly back to the twenty-first century!

Stories of Jahanpanah

Was Muhammad bin Tughlak really a 'mad genius' as he has been called, or was he a thinker far ahead of his time? The annals of history abound with his many exploits, and it is said that he brought the people of Jahanpanah, including the Sufis, much grief with his bizarre ideas. There are some gripping stories about the fourth city of Delhi.

A Traumatic Journey

It was the hot summer of 1327 CE when Muhammad bin Tughlaq decided to shift his capital from Jahanpanah to Devagiri, which he renamed Daulatabad. This invincible fort city lay more than a thousand kilometres to the south, a long journey of forty days.

Everyone was ordered to leave the capital city of Jahanpanah. 'When the sultan did this, every inhabitant left the town, abandoning furniture and possessions, and the city remained utterly deserted,' wrote Ziauddin Barani, the chronicler of the Tughlaqs, in *Tarikh-i-Firuz Shahi*, his detailed account of the Delhi sultanate, which is often considered a treasure trove of information on the period. It was said that even dogs and cats were not spared the gruelling move! Barani went on to describe how the sultan ordered his soldiers to search for anyone who had stayed behind. They found two men in the streets, a disabled man and a blind man. It is said that the enraged sultan ordered the unfortunate disabled man to be flung from a catapult and the blind man to be dragged all the way from Delhi to Daulatabad.

'One night, the sultan climbed on to the roof of his palace and looked out over Delhi. There was neither fire nor smoke nor lamp, and he said, *Now my mind is tranquil and my wrath appeased,*' Ziauddin Barani wrote.

Although the sultan built broad roads with shady trees and rest houses with amenities all along the way to Daulatabad for the citizens, many died of starvation or sheer exhaustion en route.

However, the unpopular move was a short-lived one, and Jahanpanah didn't remain abandoned for long. Eight years later, the sultan commanded the inhabitants to move back to Jahanpanah, and the capital was shifted once again. Yet, for a long time, neither the city nor its unhappy people recovered from this drastic uprooting.

'Many, from the toils of the long journey, perished on the road; and those who arrived at Devagiri could not endure the pain of exile. They pined to death in despondency,' wrote Ziauddin Barani. According to him, not even a 'thousandth part' of the original population returned to the old city.

Muhammad bin Tughlak

This reckless experiment of the sultan had proved a costly one indeed. However, most modern historians tend to believe that many of these stories were gross exaggerations, although it is true that Jahanpanah suffered a great decline in stature and trade.

A Mint in Every Household

Sultan Muhammad bin Tughlak's strange ideas invariably wreaked havoc on his people, often being original and too far ahead of their time.

He was the first in India to issue token money. When his empire was threatened with a severe drought along with frequent revolts, his coffers felt the strain. The sultan found it difficult to maintain a large supply of gold (*dinars*) and silver (*adlis*) coins. So, he introduced a token-currency system and minted vast quantities of new copper and brass coins (*tankas*) that could be exchanged for fixed amounts of gold and silver. He ordered that these be considered at par with silver and gold coins, which were kept reserved for the local treasury.

However, the new coins lacked any artistic finish, and there were no measures taken to keep the design secure and protected. They merely had some inscribed inscriptions with no royal seals stamped on them, which made the crude-looking coins easy to forge. As a result, a mint opened in every household! Soon enough, the value of these coins decreased, and it was said that they became 'as worthless as stones'. People began to hoard gold and silver coins.

The experiment failed completely, and the token currency had to be withdrawn. The sultan now had to compensate people's fake coins, which lay in large unwanted heaps, with silver coins from his treasury. It is said that, for many years, mounds of worthless copper and brass coins, rejected by the government, remained piled outside the royal fort. The royal treasury suffered crippling losses, leading to economic chaos and public resentment all round.

Muhammad bin Tughlak orders piles of brass coins to pass for silver

A Disastrous Dream

It was during the transfer of the capital from Delhi to Daulatabad that the dreaded Mongols almost plundered their way right up to Delhi. The north-western frontiers had been left neglected, and it was only with the greatest difficulty that the Mongols were driven back.

The sultan is believed to have had a grand dream of conquering Khorasan, in Central Asia, and China, to secure the western and northern frontiers of his empire. The unstable political conditions in Central Asia may have encouraged him to try to annex these areas, and he enticed nobles from these regions with grants. He managed to raise a huge cavalry of about 3,00,000 horses, which he kept barracked near his capital.

However, historians say that he neither checked the ability of the soldiers, nor the quality of the horses acquired. They were paid a year's salary in advance. After being kept idle for a whole year, the sultan found it difficult to keep paying them and decided to disband his vast cavalry. Ultimately, Muhammad bin Tughlak incurred crushing financial losses, and his reputation as a ruler and conqueror suffered.

A few years later, he sent his army to cross the Himalayas to invade China. However, it faced stiff resistance from the local Rajput raja of Kangra in the Kulu-Kangra region of modern-day Himachal Pradesh, and was forced to retreat. His huge army found it impossible to fight in the rainy and mountainous region, and nearly all of his 10,000 soldiers perished when the Kangra Rajputs closed the mountain passes, firmly blocking their passage for retreat, and hurled boulders and felled trees from the heights on the retreating army. Historians tell us how only ten cavalrymen returned to the capital to tell the sultan their sorry and humiliating tale. They were subsequently executed by the enraged sultan.

Chirag Dilli: The Light of Delhi

The sultans of Delhi usually viewed the venerated Sufi saints as a threat because of the latter's great popularity with the people and did their utmost to undermine their influence. When Ghiyasuddin Tughlak attempted to stop construction at the *baoli* of Hazrat Nizamuddin Auliya, even forbidding the supply of oil for work by night, the master remained unperturbed. He ordered his devoted disciple, the mystic poet, Nasiruddin Mahmud, to light the oil lamps with water from the water tank.

It is believed that Nasiruddin took a palmful of water and, dipping a cotton wick into it, lit it instantly. Soon all the lamps glowed brightly, and work resumed. The Auliya honoured his disciple with the title *Roshan Chiragh-e-Dehlavi*, or the 'Light of Delhi', for this miracle.

It is also said that one day, when Nasiruddin entered a religious gathering of his master and other Sufis, he did not want to sit where he was asked to sit. It would mean showing his back to some of those gathered. However, Nizamuddin Auliya countered his disciple's objection with a wise argument, saying, 'A *chiragh* has no back; it sheds its light in all directions.'

And so it was that Nasiruddin Mahmud came to be known by the title of Nasiruddin *Chiragh-e-Dehlavi*. He eventually succeeded the Auliya to become the head of the Chishti Sufis. Although Hazrat Nizamuddin's brilliant and devoted disciple, Amir Khusro, may have been a contender for the mantle of the Chishti order, Nasiruddin became the chosen one. As Hazrat Nizamuddin Auliya himself explained, 'My heart desires Amir, but Allah desires Nasiruddin.'

Khwaja Nasiruddin Chiragh-e-Dehlavi proved to be an efficient successor and spread the teachings of the Chishti Sufi order far and wide, even though he was the last of the Chishti saints in Delhi.

Muslim scholars often considered song and music as un-Islamic, even if they were used to invoke the divine. Unlike his spiritual master Nizamuddin Auliya who loved listening to *sama*, or the recitation of holy songs, Khwaja Nasiruddin did not encourage the use of instruments, music or *qawwali*. However, a poet at heart, he composed moving poetry in Persian, and it was greatly admired by all.

Muhammad bin Tughlak initially attempted, to enlist the services of the Muslim divines and the Sufis, but they always refused any association with his administration. The great popularity and influence of the Chishti sect under Hazrat Nasiruddin Chiragh-e-Dehlavi aroused the Sultan's ire and suspicion. He was said to have appointed Hazrat Nasiruddin as his attendant, and would harass him despite his devout and upright nature. The saint tolerated this treatment gracefully. On one occasion, the sultan provided food for Hazrat Nasiruddin in precious gold and silverware to test his Sufi principles. The saint simply poured some soup from the gold bowl into his palm and drank it thus.

When the sultan ordered the entire population of Jahanpanah to migrate to Daulatabad, the old capital city – which was by then a renowned centre of Islamic learning – became an abandoned ghost town. This dislocation disrupted the highly integrated organization of the Chishti Sufis, who had their centre here. They never recovered from this mighty blow.

All his life, Nasiruddin Chiragh had always preferred the seclusion of the jungle, and the village of Chiragh-e-Dehlavi grew around his dwelling amid wilderness. After his death, he was buried where he lived, and the new sultan of Delhi, Firoz Shah Tughlak, built a shrine in his memory here, in 1358 CE.

Over time, the area came to be known as Chirag Dilli. The name continues to this day, and Chirag Dilli is one of the oldest sections of South Delhi. Enclosed within the ramparts of a fort wall with four gateways, the shrine of Chirag Dilli is a venerated centre of pilgrimage for people of all faiths. Even now, in deference to the Khwaja's beliefs, no *qawwali* is performed here.

The light that once glowed in this small village has been replaced by the dazzling neon lights of its busy commercial area and the headlights of vehicles that ply on the roads around Greater Kailash and the traffic-infested Chirag Dilli flyover. Yet, the shrine that stands in the shadow of a grand *khirni* tree (*Manilkara hexandra*), said to have been planted by the Khwaja himself over 650 years ago, is a rare oasis of calm amid the bustle

Grand old *khirni* tree of Chirag Dilli *dargah*

of the narrow alleyways around. This glossy-leaved tree bears small white flowers along its branches and, to the great delight of the neighbourhood children, the fruit ripens by summer. It is also believed to have healing properties. In the summer months, earthen pots filled with water are placed around its trunk. The tree occupies pride of place in the courtyard of the *dargah*, and is arguably Delhi's most ancient tree.

Timeline:
1351–1388 CE

6

The Fifth City Firozabad Takes Shape

A Sultan's New Capital

The new sultan inherited a royal mess! When Firoz Shah Tughlak seated himself on the throne of Delhi after the death of Muhammad bin Tughlak, for the first year of his reign he was kept busy undoing the enormous muddle his cousin had created. Thanks to Muhammad bin Tughlak's disastrous policies, he inherited almost empty coffers and a disintegrating empire.

The new sultan abandoned Jahanpanah altogether. He moved four or five miles north-east of Siri to construct Firozabad, his new capital, on the west banks of the Yamuna, near the ancient Indraprastha. This was the first city to be built on the River Yamuna, to solve the constant problem of acute water scarcity faced by both Tughlakabad and Jahanpanah. And so Firozabad became the fifth city of Delhi.

Historians are not sure of the exact extent of the city of Firozabad, but it covered a part of what is now New Delhi, and included the walled city that grew around it, perhaps extending from Hauz Khas, up to and around the Ridge to the north.

History remembers Firoz Shah mostly as a zealous builder. The city was provided with canals, wells, free hospitals, schools and mosques. The *kotla*, literally meaning fortress, was the inner citadel of Firozabad. It included three splendid palaces, green gardens, the Jami Masjid and a circular *baoli*, the only one of its kind in Delhi. An Ashoka pillar brought from Topara was also re-erected here in Firoz Shah Kotla. Another Ashoka pillar, brought from Meerut, was installed near his hunting lodge at Kushk-i-Shikar on the Ridge.

The sultan's prime minister, Junan Shah Tilangani, was just as active a builder. He built seven large mosques, often considered architectural wonders, in and around Delhi. These included the Jami Masjid in the *kotla*. The Khirki Masjid or Mosque of Windows near the southern edge of Jahanpanah had red sandstone windows from which it (and, later, the locality) got its name 'Khirki'. The imposing Begumpuri Masjid stands a short distance away.

West gate of Firoz Shah Kotla, now destroyed

Firoz Shah was a keen hunter and built several hunting lodges in the forests of the Ridge. Among these lodges, the Bhooli Bhatiyari Ka Mahal, Pir Ghaib and Malcha Mahal still survive, and are shrouded in spooky folklore. The sultan and his courtiers would also visit the Shikargah or Kushk Mahal, constructed in the wilderness. They would live here for a couple of days at a time, while hunting in the area around, which probably teemed with wildlife like leopards, nilgai and various species of deer.

The sultan even rebuilt the top storey of the Qutb Minar, which had been struck by lightning. He replaced the fallen storey with two new ones and a cupola (small dome) at the summit in marble and sandstone. This keen builder also reconstructed Alauddin's Hauz-i-Alai, which had fallen into neglect. He had the tank cleared and built a college for the study of Arabic at one end. This became a centre of Islamic learning, and its fame spread far and wide. Firoz Shah called the complex 'Hauz Khas', meaning 'special water tank'.

Unlike his predecessors, Firoz Shah did not try to extend the frontiers of his empire. In fact, he didn't even attempt to reclaim areas that had broken away. He worked towards improving the infrastructure of his kingdom by building hospitals, schools, canals, rest houses and reservoirs. He is said to be the first ruler to introduce canal irrigation in India and even built the biggest network of canals to bring more land under cultivation. In fact, the well-being of his subjects was the hallmark of his reign.

Unlike Tughlakabad, Firozabad lacked defensive construction and, after the collapse of the Tughlak Empire, the Mongol invader Timur found it an easy target. He plundered the riches of the citadel, leaving behind ruined structures. These were

again ravaged and reused by Shahjahan for the construction of Shahjahanabad, the seventh and last city of ancient Delhi.

Once standing tall on the banks of the River Yamuna, which has long since changed its course, most of the *kotla* now lies in ruins. All one can see are the shells of destroyed buildings, exposed subterranean passages and stumps that were once pillars in magnificent palaces and halls. A few structures with pyramidal roofs also form a part of the ruins. The 13-metre-high Ashoka

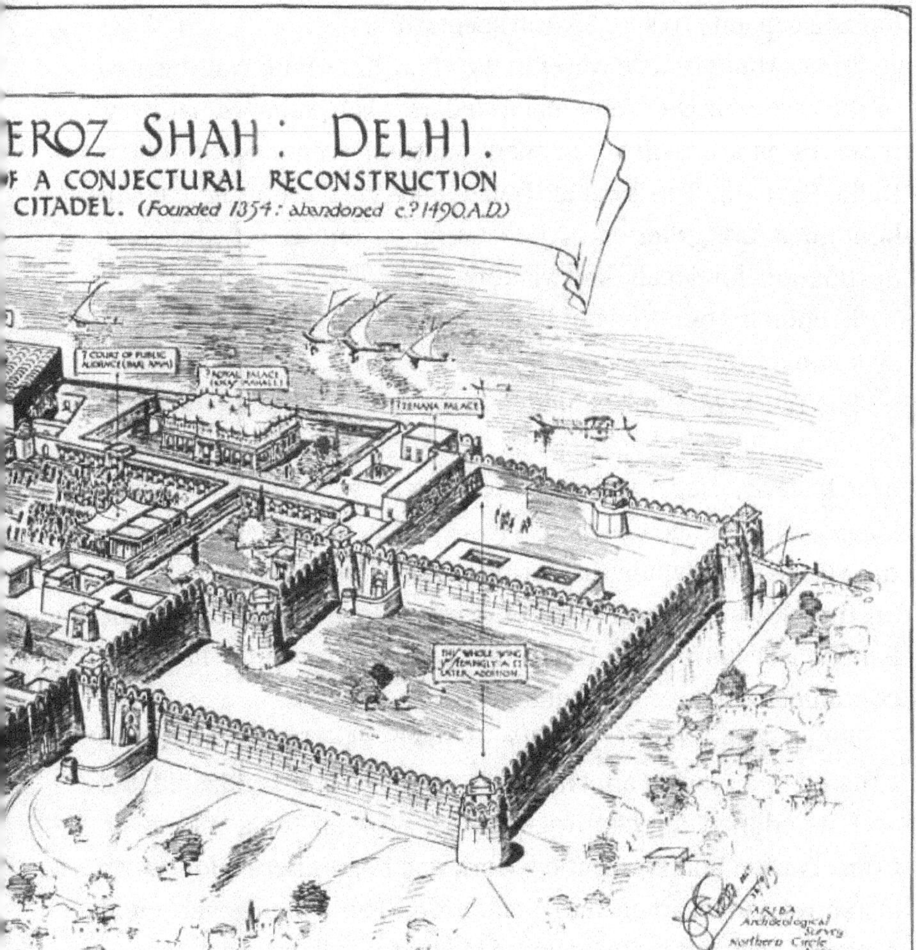

pillar which Firoz Shah had brought from Topara, still rises from the palace's ruins here. The Jami Masjid is in use even though its prayer hall is derelict, but huge crowds gather on Thursdays at the *kotla* to offer prayers.

Everyone is familiar with the Firoz Shah Kotla Cricket Stadium, now renamed Arun Jaitley Stadium, the famed venue of international and domestic cricket matches in Delhi. Located just a few yards away, off Bahadur Shah Zafar Marg, between Old and New Delhi, it is one of the oldest cricket stadiums in India and has the capacity to seat 55,000 spectators.

Today, there is little water in the Hauz Khas tank, but the area of the reservoir is evident, encircled as it is by a paved pathway. It serves as a backdrop for many cultural events organized by Delhi Tourism. The swanky Hauz Khas Village houses elegant boutiques, art galleries and restaurants, and is a fashionable destination for locals and visitors alike. The landscaped Deer Park, home to hundreds of birds and spotted deer, is also easily accessible from here.

The Khirki Masjid lies hidden away behind a huddle of shops facing the fancy shopping malls of Saket. The Begumpuri Masjid near Malaviya Nagar is Delhi's second largest mosque after Jama Masjid, with a huge courtyard. It served as a refugee shelter for the villagers of Begumpur during Nadir Shah's brutal onslaught on the city in the eighteenth century. Once again, during the Partition of 1947, many Hindu families sought shelter here and continued to stay on until quite recently.

Firoz Shah's hunting lodge, known as Malcha Mahal, is situated deep inside a forest in Chanakyapuri. It lay dilapidated and abandoned for centuries, but is now up for a makeover. Conservation and restoration work has begun here, along with attractive landscaping and plantation. The Delhi government plans to include it in its 'haunted heritage walks' route.

Another of the sultan's favourite hunting lodges, the Shikargah or Kushk Mahal, nestles amid the trees within the Teen Murti

Bhavan complex, once the residence of India's first prime minister, Jawaharlal Nehru, and in front of the Nehru Planetarium, library and auditorium. This is now known as the Prime Ministers' Library and Museum Society, depicting the lives and times of all of India's prime ministers since independence. The nearby Kushak Road is named after the sultan's hunting lodge, Kushk Mahal. And close by, a main arterial road is called Tughlak Road after this dynasty.

It's quite unimaginable that this prime area of central Delhi, perhaps India's most elite residential location today, housing the country's most powerful people – the prime minister, cabinet ministers and bureaucrats – once lay in wilderness and teemed with wildlife!

Remains of buildings at Firoz Shah Kotla, Delhi, 1795

City of Djinns and Pirs

Did djinns or ghosts actually live in Firoz Shah's fifth city? And do they still lurk there? Weird stories abound around many of Firozabad's forgotten ruins; about haunted nooks and spooky corners. These have challenged the faithful as well as the daredevils to venture here today and find out for themselves!

The Djinns of Firoz Shah Kotla

Who or what are djinns?

According to Islamic mythology and popular belief, they are supernatural creatures made of smokeless fire, who make their homes in abandoned places. These spirits are said to tend to the faithful who seek help.

Sultan Firoz Shah, it is said, was fond of meeting dervishes, holy men and Sufi saints who lived in his sultanate. After his death and the dissolution of his empire, it was believed that djinns continued to inhabit the ruins of Firoz Shah Kotla for over five centuries, right down to this day! Indeed, it is now known as a 'haunted citadel' or 'City of Djinns'.

In fairly recent times, about five decades ago, the underground chambers of this fortress developed a curious reputation as being the abode of spirits to whom petitions could be written and who had to be appeased.

So, every Thursday, hordes of visitors, irrespective of religion, visit the ruins of the ancient citadel. Strangely, these visitors are not tourists or picnickers, but devotees seeking the blessings of djinns.

They come carrying copies of letters, citing their problems – property disputes, family concerns, sickness, missing relatives, job matters, marriage decisions, or even evil spirits... They firmly believe that there is a solution here for every problem and that their wishes will be granted. They stick the letters on various strategic spots of the citadel and offer prayers to the djinns, lighting candles, *diyas* and incense, offering milk, fruit and grain, coloured threads and bits of cloth. Many swear that their problems have been resolved. As soon as that happens, they return to distribute sweets or biryani to the people around.

Letters to the 'djinns' at Firoz Shah Kotla

Another popular belief here is that the chief of the Kotla Djinns, Laat Waale Baba, lives in the *laat* or Ashoka pillar here. Letters written to him are tied to the railing around the pillar. If you can manage to reach through the railing and touch the pillar, it is believed your wish will be fulfilled!

An old legend tells us that the Sikh Guru Tegh Bahadur Singh was held captive at the *kotla* by Aurangzeb in the seventeenth century CE, without food or water. However, when the emperor's soldiers returned a week later, expecting to see him emaciated and weak, he looked healthy and happy. The djinns had apparently looked after him well!

Standing atop this ancient fortress in the heart of the bustle of Delhi, there is, perhaps, an ethereal ambience to the rubble and ruins of Feroz Shah Kotla. Or is it simply one's imagination playing strange tricks?

The Golden Minar of Topara

It was during a hunting expedition around Delhi that Firoz Shah Tughlak came across two Ashokan pillars – one in Topara, in the Yamunanagar district, and the other in Meerut. They had been installed there by the famous Mauryan king, Ashoka, in the third century BCE. However, nobody was sure of this, since it had taken place over 1,600 years before. The sultan was told that the pillars had been standing here since the days of the Pandavas. What is more, they were rumoured to be the *laat* or walking sticks of Bhim, the mighty Pandava. It was even said that Bhima had used the two sticks together to herd cattle!

The sultan's curiosity was instantly aroused! According to Shams-i-Sirak Afif, a chronicler of the time and the ruler's close friend, who would accompany the sultan on his hunting expeditions, Firoz Shah Tughlak, a great lover of architecture, was filled with the greatest admiration. He resolved to remove the two pillars to his capital as trophies and a memorial for future generations. Perhaps he was thinking of the iconic Iron Pillar that stood near the Qutb Minar.

The Topara pillar sets sail for Firozabad

However, the pillars were not easy to transport for they were gigantic, unwieldy and heavy structures in polished sandstone, each about 13 metres tall. The sultan summoned thousands of soldiers and commanded the people in Topara to move the pillar standing here.

It was a huge effort! The pillar was carefully cut into segments and wrapped in silk cotton before being lowered on to a soft bed of reeds and raw hides and then placed on a forty-two-wheel carriage. Strong ropes were attached to each wheel and then 200 men hauled the carriage all the way to the Yamuna bank, from where it was freighted to Firozabad in large boats. This was an arduous journey of over 200 kilometres!

Another massive operation followed when the pillar was erected in the heart of the *kotla*, at the top of a pyramid-shaped, three-tier palace pavilion. This was constructed especially to support this colossal pillar. The pinkish pillar glowed golden in the sunlight, its original Mauryan polish untarnished. It came to be called the Minara-e-Zarrin or the Golden Minar.

The sultan was puzzled by the strange writing inscribed at the base of the Topara pillar. Many learned scholars were summoned, but nobody could decipher it as it was in the ancient Brahmi script. Thus, the sultan never got to understand the message on the relic.

Inscriptions engraved on pillar

It took five centuries to reveal the secret of the Topara pillar when an English scholar, James Princep, translated the writing with the help of scripts on other pillars and rocks. Now, at last, one could make sense of the mysterious engravings! Princep helped the world learn more about King Ashoka's reign, and established that King Devanampriya, meaning 'beloved of the gods', or Piyadasi, meaning 'he who regards others with kindness', as mentioned in several inscriptions, was none other than King Ashoka!

The inscriptions engraved on the stone pillars described King Ashoka's edicts of Dharma. The king wanted these edicts to endure far into the distant ages in posterity – for as long as the sun and moon lasted! He urged his people to lead a just and correct life. The king disclosed here that he had planted shady fig trees along the highways for the benefit of both men and animals. He also mentioned that he would like the generations after him to follow

Ashokan pillar from Topara at Firoz Shah Kotla

his benevolent acts towards everybody in society – parents, spiritual teachers, the aged and orphans, as well as helpers and the destitute. He also wished religion to be compassionate, free of persecution or sacrifice of any living beings.

The Vanishing Saint of Pir Ghaib

Firoz Shah, the master builder, built several hunting lodges in the forests of the Ridge, which were rich with wildlife. He constructed a hunting lodge called Kushk-i-Shikar, or the 'Palace of the Hunt', on a high ridge in the wilderness. It was also known as the Kushk-i-Jahan-Numa, or the 'Palace with a View of the World', perhaps because of its splendid bird's-eye view of his capital city, stretching out far south of the River Yamuna. The two-storey hunting lodge, along with an enclosure for game animals, was

built by the sultan probably after the death of his favourite son, Fateh Khan, to help distract himself through hunting.

Interestingly, it may have also served as an astronomical observatory, and this could also tie up with its name. There are circular holes in the roof of the building on the first and second floors, and a cylindrical structure on the roof directly above the hole. What were they used for? Had there been a clock tower here? Nobody knows for sure. We do know, however,

Firoz Shah Kotla *baoli*

that the sultan himself was keenly interested in astronomy, and astrological charts were drawn up during his reign. New systems were also developed to measure time.

A second Ashokan pillar, 33 feet tall and made of red sandstone, was laboriously sailed down the River Yamuna from Meerut on big boats by Firoz Shah, just as he had done with the Topara pillar. This was installed at the hunting lodge with great ceremony. This pillar was also engraved with Ashokan inscriptions and gleamed in the sunlight. However, today it has a rough exterior and its inscriptions have eroded. And it's no surprise why! It broke into five pieces in the eighteenth century during an explosion, and for the next 150 years the pieces just lay around on the ground here. The pillar was later restored by Kolkata's Asiatic Society and returned to its original location here on a double-stepped platform.

A stepwell or *baoli* built next to the hunting lodge by the sultan was probably a bathing area and a water-recharge point, as well as the only source of water in this area. The *baoli* originally included a tunnel, which is no longer accessible.

Later, the name of the Kushk was changed to Pir Ghaib, which literally means the 'vanishing saint'. A mysterious story lies behind this name.

It is said that the sultan once climbed the steep, winding staircase of his hunting lodge and, to his surprise, found a Sufi saint meditating in one of the two rooms. When he looked closer, he was startled to find it unoccupied. The fakir had disappeared mysteriously! Nobody had seen him leave. Had he drawn an invisible veil around himself? Soon after, he reappeared to the sultan in a dream and said, 'I keep coming here; do remember me.'

The sultan and his courtiers all found great peace at the hunting lodge, and so they began to visit it frequently. The place came to be known as Pir Ghaib, in honour of the Sufi saint whom he had encountered here.

Today, the monument of Pir Ghaib, as it is still known, is a largely forgotten ruin standing in the heart of the northern ridge of Delhi, on the edge of the sprawling campus of the Bara Hindu Rao Hospital. However, it has a mysterious air about it and, even now, people come here to pray. They light incense sticks and offer flowers to the 'vanishing saint'. Perhaps they hope to get lucky and catch a glimpse him!

The *baoli* here was said to be the only source of water for the British officers and soldiers during the 1857 War of Indian Independence. Apprehensive that the rebelling Indian soldiers might poison its waters, the British Army had stationed a guard in the area permanently. Today, the *baoli* has little water, and is

The ruins of Pir Ghaib

mostly choked with garbage and overgrown shrubs. There is a proposal to clean it up and recharge it through water harvesting.

The Ashoka pillar remains standing nearby, between Bara Hindu Rao Hospital and Mutiny Memorial. The building's observatory has also deeply interested astronomers. They feel that this monument might possibly be India's oldest surviving astronomical observatory, dating back to the fourteenth century.

Timeline:
1388–1526 CE

7

Delhi's Darkest Days

A Tumultuous Time

As it happened all too often in Indian history, hatred and fratricide proved to be the undoing of the great Tughlak Empire. Bitter civil war followed the death of Firoz Shah Tughlak, which reduced the once mighty sultanate to Punjab and Delhi alone.

And then came the fearful Tamarlane or Timur, the Mongol-Turkish warrior from Central Asia, who claimed to be a descendant of Genghis Khan. Nicknamed the 'Prince of Destruction', he was the epitome of cruelty, looting and razing everything that stood in his path to the ground. In just four months, he travelled, practically unopposed, to Delhi from Samarkand, the capital of the Mongol Empire, and unleashed his warriors upon the hapless city in a maelstrom of butchery and plunder. This was the final blow to the tottering Delhi sultanate.

Timur

Those were dark days indeed for the mighty imperial capital. Its population was mercilessly massacred and the city ransacked bare. The Tughlak dynasty crumbled along with its capital city. This was one of Timur's greatest victories as, at the time, Delhi was one of the richest cities in the world. Tragically, Delhi was ravaged and reduced to a city of rubble, as Timur carried away with him elephants loaded with tons of treasure, costly building materials and even prized artists, masons and skilled workers as prisoners. The city faded into oblivion in the fifteenth century.

It is said that it took a long, long while, almost a century, for Delhi to recover from this death blow. And when it did so, it was no longer the capital of a great empire. Timur's thunderbolt had splintered the empire into shards, and northern India remained weak and divided as newer kingdoms emerged.

Gradually, the Sayyid dynasty, who claimed to be *sayyids*, or descendants of the Prophet Muhammad, succeeded the Tughlaks and ruled the Delhi sultanate for about thirty-seven years, until they were displaced by the Lodis.

The Lodi dynasty, founded by Bahlul Lodi, a powerful Punjab chief, was the fifth and last ruling family of the Delhi sultanate, and the only dynasty of Afghan origin.

The Lodis asserted their authority over much of the north, and vigorously set about the mammoth task of reconstructing the Delhi sultanate and restoring it to its old glory. Sikandar Lodi, son of Bahlul Lodi, proved to be a capable ruler who expanded the Lodi territory into the regions of present-day Gwalior and Bihar. He was a patron of learning, as also a poet of repute, but an orthodox Muslim.

In 1504, Sikandar Lodi founded the city of Agra to become his capital. The village of Sikandra, near Agra, where the tomb of Akbar stands, was named after him. And so, the capital city of Delhi was forsaken once again, and it fell into a deep shadow of neglect. However, when a devastating earthquake shook north India and Delhi in 1505, damaging the Qutb Minar, Sikandar Lodi repaired it without delay.

Sikandar's youngest son, Ibrahim Lodi, was the last Lodi sultan of Delhi. An autocratic and suspicious tyrant, he faced several rebellions during most of his reign, because his harshness towards his nobles and officials had built discontent everywhere. In fact, he alienated them to such an extent that the governor of Punjab, Daulat Khan Lodi, invited the Mughal ruler of Kabul,

Timur defeats the sultan of Delhi

Babur, a descendant of Timur, to invade India. This was the nemesis of Lodi rule in the country !

Despite his vast army, Ibrahim was defeated and killed by Babur's invading forces in 1526 at the First Battle of Panipat. This historic battle, fought on the level plains of Panipat about 100 kilometres north of Delhi, marked the end of the Lodi dynasty and indeed the Delhi sultanate. With the rise of the Mughal Empire led by Babur, the destiny of Delhi was to change momentously yet again.

Imagine living through those uncertain times in Delhi! It was, as you can imagine, a tumultuous and turbulent time for the masses, who lived in insecurity and fear with the arrival of the invaders, and the several changes in dynasties and sultans.

However, there was a silver lining round the corner. The period now saw the beginnings of the Bhakti movement in north India, a religious reform movement that acted as a healing balm. Many saints – Hindu, Muslim and Sikh – spread the message of total devotion to the divine through their poetry and teachings. They believed that God is universal, and condemned religious rituals, idol worship and social inequality. The saints of the Bhakti movement – like Lalleshwari, Ramananda, Kabir, Guru Nanak and others, along with the Sufi saints – spread the message of tolerance, peace and friendship in the language of the common people.

The people of Delhi were already familiar with the teachings of the Sufi saints, many of whom had lived here right from the time of Qutbuddin Bakhtiyar Kaki to Nizamuddin Auliya and his successor, Chirag-i-Dehlavi, and their disciples. The Bhakti movement's influence spread to Delhi, where saints such as Guru Nanak and subsequent Sikh gurus arrived to preach and uplift the downtrodden masses. They embraced a simpler approach to devotion and religious understanding. The movement sought to reduce the bitterness between communities, and lay the foundations of a liberal, tolerant and inclusive society with high moral values.

Tomb of Sikandar Lodi

The tombs of the Sayyid and Lodi rulers stand in what was once the village of Khairpur in the heart of today's Delhi. Built in the Indo-Islamic architectural style, they lie scattered in the beautiful Lodi Gardens, a green haven extending over 90 acres on the main Lodi Road, between Khan Market and Safdarjung's Tomb.

Here, among other structures, the Bara Gumbad Mosque, with its big dome, and the Shisha Gumbad, often known as the Glass Dome, with a turquoise blue façade, enhance the serene beauty of this historical park.

During the reign of Akbar, a beautiful stone bridge with arches and pillars, known as Atthpula or Eight-Piered bridge, was constructed across a small lake here. The lush gardens are a major attraction for lovers of history and nature, and heritage walks are also conducted here. Fountains, jogging tracks, a glasshouse and a National Bonsai Park attract people here in great numbers as do its popular shaded picnic spots.

The Darkness Is Illuminated

The Delhi sultanate had been scarred severely by Timur's bloody carnage, and continued to witness anarchy as every few years there was a new sultan and a fresh tussle for the throne. Yet, remarkable stories of figures of faith and devotion helped overpower the gloom of those troubled times.

Guru Nanak Visits Delhi

It was a time of darkness and upheaval when the revered saint and the first Sikh guru, Guru Nanak, visited Delhi.

During his lifetime, Guru Nanak witnessed the rule of five Muslim rulers: Bahlol Lodi, Sikandar Lodi, Ibrahim Lodi, Babur and Humayun. It was against this backdrop of instability that the guru travelled far and wide to many parts of India and West Asia, to spread his holy message of peace, equality and compassion to all of mankind. His message was simple, powerful and universal:

> There is but one God; Truth His name; the Creator; beyond fear; beyond hate.
> Timeless; beyond the cycle of birth and death; Self-existent;
> Realized by the grace of the true guru.

He was true in the beginning, true through the ages, and is true here and now,
O Nanak, forever and ever true.

– Opening words of the Guru Granth Sahib,
the holy book of the Sikhs

It was during the hot summer of 1505, during the reign of Sikandar Lodi, that Guru Nanak visited Delhi with his long-time Muslim companion, Bhai Mardana. The people of Delhi flocked in large numbers to the garden where he was camping to meet him, and to listen to his inspiring sermons and *kirtan*. They made him many precious offerings, which Guru Nanak distributed to

Guru Nanak

the poor and needy. He also fed community meals or *langar* to all regardless of religion, caste or gender. The camping site was called '*piao*' as Guru Nanak himself served cool water to thirsty travellers from a deep well that he had arranged to have dug here. Gradually, several monks and holy people started visiting the site to hold religious discussions with the saint.

A story goes that, while Guru Nanak was staying at the camp, he saw some people weeping bitterly. He asked them the cause of their sorrow. They told him that their elephant had died. He demonstrated to them that the elephant was not dead but merely asleep. When they saw their elephant slowly come back to life, they prostrated themselves at the guru's feet.

One day, it is said, the favourite elephant of Sultan Sikandar Lodi died. He had heard of the miracle performed by Guru Nanak and promptly sent for him, requesting him to revive his royal elephant. The guru replied that life and death were in the hands of the Almighty, and that one should accept and rejoice in His will. An ordinary human being like him could not interfere with His will.

This enraged the sultan so much that he immediately imprisoned the guru. He also banned his public preaching. Here, in prison, Guru Nanak was asked to grind corn, using grinding stones. Guru Nanak sat down and started singing his hymns. It is believed that, after a while, people saw the grinding stones move on their own to complete his work. Everyone present in the prison room bowed their heads, knowing that they were witnessing a great miracle.

The guru's deep compassion for the suffering of other prisoners and his message of spiritual harmony influenced the prison officials greatly. They informed the sultan that Guru Nanak deeply respected all people and religions.

While he was in prison, it is said that a great earthquake shook Delhi. 'The mountains were overturned, and lofty edifices were dashed to the ground. The living thought the Day of Judgment had come for them, and for the dead, the Day of Resurrection,' a chronicler of the times wrote.

It was widely believed that the sultan's offensive behaviour had caused the guru to curse the city. Meanwhile, the Chishti Sufi saints and prison officials intervened, and Sultan Sikandar Lodi finally ordered the release of Guru Nanak along with many other prisoners, upon the guru's request.

Many years later, the place where the first Sikh guru had camped in a garden in Delhi became the site for a gurdwara made of white marble, Gurdwara Nanak Piao. The garden around the gurdwara grew into a place of pilgrimage for people from all over Delhi, for this is where they had first received the message of spiritual deliverance from the saint.

Today, the imposing gurdwara in white marble, with a gold-plated dome, stands on Rana Pratap Road, also known as Grand Trunk Road or GT Road, near North Delhi's Sabzi Mandi area, the location of a wholesale vegetable-and-fruit market. The gurdwara is now a revered historical shrine. The well from which the guru served water still stands and has been kept well-maintained amid beautiful gardens. Special programmes at the gurdwara are held to mark the birth and death anniversaries of Guru Nanak, apart from several other festive occasions of the Sikh community.

The Hillock of Majnu

During the reign of Sultan Sikandar Lodi, a Sufi hermit from Iran called Abdulla, was said to have lived a secluded life on the right bank of the River Yamuna where it flows through Delhi. He would help ferry people across the river in his small boat, free of charge, as a service to God.

His desire to see God was so great that he was always lost in his own thoughts, often starving himself. He became reed thin.

People nicknamed him 'Majnu' after the well-known Persian lover who was a symbol of intense love and passion. Deeply engrossed in the divine, Majnu would sit in meditation day after day, oblivious to the world around him.

One day, Guru Nanak was walking along the riverbank when he came upon Majnu. He gave the emaciated, rag-clad hermit his blessings. He told him that it was not essential to fast or live so austerely to reach God. One could lead a normal life and yet be close to Him.

With the blessings of Guru Nanak, Majnu is believed to have attained the enlightenment he had so long sought, and he became his devout disciple. His hermitage came to be known as Majnu Ka Tilla, or the 'Hillock of Majnu'.

Guru Nanak stayed with him at his hermitage for many days. He was so pleased with Majnu's dedication that he blessed his new devotee and told him that his name would be immortalized. Many more people were attracted to the hermitage by Majnu's divine personality and his dedicated love for his guru.

While Guru Nanak was camping on this hillock, many Sufi saints of Delhi came to meet him and hold discussions with him here. They included the spiritual leader of the shrine of Hazrat Nizamuddin Auliya, who was deeply influenced by his discourse with Guru Nanak.

Many years later, after the torture and death of his father, the fifth Sikh guru, Guru Arjan Dev, the sixth Sikh guru, Guru Hargobind, also stayed at this humble hermitage in 1612 when Emperor Jahangir invited him to Delhi. The emperor, suspicious of his growing influence, had him imprisoned at Gwalior Fort, although he was released later. The guru, however, insisted that fifty-two Hindu kings, who had been imprisoned there, be released as well. This event came to be celebrated by the Sikhs on Diwali day with fireworks and lights as Bandi Chhor Diwas. The guru stayed at Majnu Ka Tilla a second time on his way back to the Punjab. The later Sikh gurus often held their religious discourses

Majnu Ka Tilla Gurdwara

here as well, and the shrine became a centre of historical importance in the coming years.

In later history, Sikh military leader, Sardar Baghel Singh Dhaliwal, also camped at the hillock in 1783, and built two small structures here to commemorate the stay of Guru Nanak as also of Guru Hargobind later. In memory of the Sufi saint Majnu, the shrine was named Gurdwara Majnu Ka Tilla.

The surrounding estate was donated to the gurdwara later in the early nineteenth century by the Sikh emperor, Maharaja Ranjit Singh, for its maintenance. He also had the structures faced with marble. This tiny marble gurdwara can still be seen here today. The present Gurdwara Majnu Ka Tilla was constructed in its massive, majestic form by devotees in 1950.

Today, Majnu Ka Tilla Gurdwara is one of the oldest places of Sikh pilgrimage in Delhi and the National Capital Region. Over the centuries, it has come to immortalize the name of the devoted Majnu and his Tilla, as foretold by his guru. The birth of the Sikh order, the Khalsa, instituted by the tenth and last guru, Guru Gobind Singh, is celebrated at this gurdwara on Baisakhi with much festivity. A special *langar* or free meal from the community kitchen of the gurdwara, is arranged for the huge crowd of pilgrims, regardless of religion, caste, gender or social status.

Langars are a unique feature of all gurdwaras, where worshippers are also served *kada prasad*, or rich *atta* halwa, at all times. It is believed that the guru never sends away a devotee hungry or empty-handed. Also, the gurdwara here enthusiastically observes full-moon days.

The site of Majnu Ka Tilla Gurdwara, upon a hillock on the right bank of the River Yamuna, lies on a stretch of the National

Highway 1, part of the historic Grand Trunk Road and the Outer Ring Road of Delhi and just a stone's throw from ISBT Kashmiri Gate, in North Delhi, and the Tibetan Refugee Camp. Delhi's 'Little Tibet', as this is popularly known, is a 'hot' destination for both the young and the old, foreign tourists, the students from the North Campus of Delhi University and for others looking for a unique experience. It houses a small monastery and Buddhist temple apart from many restaurants that specialize in Tibetan cuisine and shops selling Tibetan handicrafts and curios.

Masjid Moth or the 'Lentil Mosque'

An interesting story lies behind the construction of the Masjid Moth or Lentil Mosque in the sixteenth century by Wazir Miya Bhoiya, the prime minister of Sultan Sikandar Lodi.

It is said that the minister was strolling along with the sultan in a stretch of open forest area when Sikandar Lodi suddenly bent down and picked up a grain of lentil or *moth* that had probably been dropped by a bird. He presented it with a flourish to his minister, who accepted it with a show of gratitude, although he was quite bewildered.

Wazir Miya Bhoiya spent a sleepless night, wondering what to do with the grain. To throw it away would imply disrespect to his sovereign. He reflected that a seed that had been so honoured by His Majesty ought not to be simply discarded but be used in the service of God.

Eventually, he decided to plant the grain, which grew with astonishingly speed to yield 200 grains of *moth* in its very first year! In a few years, the plant had multiplied so much that its bountiful harvest was like a *moth* revolution!

In gratitude, Wazir Miya Bhoiya decided to build a small mosque from the surplus income of the lentil harvest. He invited Sultan Sikandar Lodi to visit the mosque built from his gift.

View from outer wall of Moth Ki Masjid

The sultan was so pleased to hear the whole story that he named the mosque Moth Ki Masjid or Mosque of the Lentil. This mosque was known as the private masjid of the prime minister, Wazir Miya Bhoiya, and he spent much of his time here in prayer.

Raised on a high platform, this strikingly attractive mosque of red sandstone has a square layout. Moth Ki Masjid is built in the Indo-Islamic style of architecture and is identified by its relative simplicity of form and small size as compared to other mosques like the Begumpuri mosque. It is also different because, interestingly, it has no minarets or calligraphic decorations, which are traditional features of mosques. It has a small dome and windows with latticed screens. It is situated within the village of Masjid Moth, named after it, and can be approached from the street on the eastern side through an exquisitely designed gate made of red, blue, black and white sandstone. Elephant-trunk carvings and square pillars embellish this gate.

Moth Ki Masjid is now completely enclosed within the modern locality of South Extension Part II, Uday Park and Masjid Moth comprising urban residential and commercial establishments of upscale South Delhi. It is easily accessible by metro or local transport from Dhaula Kuan, Yusuf Sarai or the landmark AIIMS hospital. However, the mosque itself lies in a state of sad neglect with encroachments all around and garbage dumps lining the path leading up to it.

Nevertheless, Moth Ki Masjid has merged seamlessly into the life of its neighbourhood as people sit around in its courtyard where there are shady neem trees and a large, dry well. Children play cricket here or walk on its terraces until the sun goes down.

The Curious Tale of Jamali-Kamali

Sheikh Fazalullah or Jamali was a noted court poet and Sufi saint who lived through the times of Sikander Lodi, Ibrahim Lodi, Babar and even a part of Humayun's reign. His poetry mirrored the Persian mysticism of the times. It was said that his poems was so beautiful that even Sikandar Lodi, who was a renowned poet himself, used to get his literary works polished by him.

After the Mughal conquest of India, Jamali was given a place in their court and continued to enjoy the patronage of the Mughal rulers, Babur and his son Humayun. He remained here up to the time of his death.

As a young man, he led a carefree existence. The story goes that, one day, during the rainy season, he fixed a rendezvous with a friend at a secluded spot. He waited impatiently for her to arrive. Dusk was falling when at last he saw a hooded figure approach him through the drizzle. He darted out and grabbed the figure, who turned out to be a holy man and not his expected friend at all!

His life changed dramatically, it is said, and he turned into a hermit, abandoning his wild ways. He came to be known as Jalal Shah or the Fiery Saint. He was reputed to perform miracles and he demonstrated his '*jamal*' or glory everywhere, hence the name Jamali.

Before his death, he constructed his own richly ornate mosque in Mehrauli, in red sandstone and white marble, with five arches and a studded dome. He was close to Emperor Humayun in his later years and, in fact, passed away in Ahmedabad, Gujarat, when he was with him on an expedition. As Jamali had always desired to be buried next to the mosque he had built, Humayun sent his remains to Mehrauli from Gujarat. He had his tomb built adjacent to the mosque as a tribute to Jamali's beautiful poetry.

Within the main enclosure of the Jamali-Kamali complex, the tomb has two graves - one of Jamali and the other of Kamali - whose identity is yet unknown but is widely believed to be the

Archways in the Jamali-Kamali mosque

very same holy man who changed the course of Fazalullah's life. 'Kamal' in Urdu means miracle. Who Kamali really was, however, remains a mystery! Whether he was the holy man, a disciple of Jamali, or his wife, or a close companion, or another Sufi poet, no one knows for sure. The ceiling of Jamali's tomb is beautifully inscribed with quotations from the Quran, and its walls are adorned with verses from the Sufi saint's own poems.

Jamali-Kamali's monuments are located within the beautiful Mehrauli Archaeological Park, which actually shares a boundary with the Qutub Minar premises. The park stretches over 200 acres and is a historical treasure trove, housing as it does monuments like the Zafar Mahal, the tomb of Balban, mosques and stepwells, built over five centuries. A popular picnic spot today, especially during the sunny winter months, it lies just off the busy Mehrauli–Gurgaon Road.

Yet spooky stories surround the place! Is the Jamali-Kamali complex haunted? It is rumoured that the seemingly tranquil monuments are haunted by djinns who reside here. These structures were left abandoned for a long time, until the ASI took over with their restoration work in recent years. As djinns are believed to sometimes step into deserted places, they may have refused to leave, even with the arrival of the ASI, and continue to live here. When annoyed by human presence, they are alleged to slap or scare visitors to the complex with ghostly lights and sounds. People are reported to have heard laughter, whispers and even strange cries. It's little wonder then that this popular tourist attraction by day sees the crowds vanish hastily as soon as the sun begins to set!

Timeline:
1526–1627 CE

8

The Sixth City
New Beginnings at Purana Qila

The City Rises Again

The fortunes of the ancient city of Delhi were all set to change yet again! And this time, it was with the coming of the mighty Mughal dynasty, which ruled effectively over most of the Indian subcontinent for more than 300 years!

A century and a quarter after Delhi was devastated by his forefather Timur, Zahiruddin Babur was spurred by the lure of untold wealth and the story of his ancestor's triumphant invasion of the Indian subcontinent, to a new adventure here. A born leader, he believed himself to be the rightful heir to the throne of Timur, the Delhi sultanate. However, unlike his forefather, for him Hindustan was not a land for plunder. It was a homeland to be claimed and created, and a kingdom to rule.

It was a turn in the destinies of the ancient city again! This semi-nomadic warlord rode southwards from Afghanistan through the Khyber Pass, storming into north India. He won the throne of Delhi after a decisive battle with Ibrahim Lodi at Panipat in 1526.

Babur wrote about his victory in his memoirs, the *Baburnama*:

> 'By the grace of the Almighty God, this difficult task was made easy to me,
> and that mighty army, in the space of half a day, was laid in dust.'

It was the end of the Lodi era and the already tottering Delhi sultanate, as Babur went on to occupy Delhi. He proclaimed himself emperor of Hindustan and sent his son, Humayun, to seize Agra. Babur decided to make Agra his capital. Although his reign lasted only four years, this victory marked the beginning of the Mughal dynasty, which claimed its descent from the Mongols, hence the name 'Mughal'.

After the death of Babur when he was only forty-eight years old, a new capital, the sixth city of Delhi was built by both Humayun, the son of Babur, and Sher Shah Suri, the son of an Afghan adventurer of the Sur tribe who had been once recruited by Sultan Bahlol Lodi of Delhi. Sher Shah had been given the title of 'Sher', or lion, when he valiantly killed a tiger as a young man. He briefly became emperor of the whole of north India including Delhi, after he defeated Humayun on two occasions.

Babur and Humayun

Humayun started constructing his new city called *Din Panah* or 'Refuge of the Faithful', a cosmopolitan centre for the learned, wise and holy men of every religion to gather and dwell here in harmony. Sher Shah completed work on this city, which was known as Shergarh, or Purana Qila, later. So, once again, Delhi came into the limelight as it became the seat of the new empire.

It is said that a romantic streak in the dreamy Humayun made him select the site of the ancient city of Indraprastha, situated on an old mound on the banks of the River Yamuna, as the location for his new capital. Protected by the Aravalli mountain range on one side, its elevated setting next to the wide river gave it protection in case of an attack. Moreover, the site was also at a stone's throw from the shrine of Delhi's most revered saint, Nizamuddin Auliya, where kings and commoners alike sought blessings.

Work on the fort and the new city was almost over when the Afghan, Sher Shah Suri, defeated Humayun in the Battle of Chausa, near Buxar in Bihar, in 1539. The very next year, in 1540, he routed Humayun in the Battle of Kannauj, in Uttar Pradesh. The wounded Mughal emperor was forced to flee the battlefield, leaving behind his army and ammunition. He lost his kingdom and spent the next fifteen years in exile, wandering in the Indian borderlands.

Building a city was considered the ultimate sign of victory at the time. Sher Shah Suri decided to construct another city in Delhi but opted for the same site as Din Panah.

While Humayun built the body of Din Panah, it has been sometimes said that its soul was the work of Sher Shah. An enthusiastic builder, he built his new capital, the Shergarh or Purana Qila, where Humayun's Din Panah stood. Sher Shah razed to the ground most of the structures built by Humayun within the fort and replaced them with several new edifices with material from the cities of Siri and Firozabad, which were already in ruins because of frequent invasions.

Thus, the sixth city of Delhi was constructed on the very site where the magnificent Indraprastha had once stood. Sher Shah also established a vast and powerful empire and strengthened it with a wise system of administration. However, his reign was short-lived, lasting only five years.

It took Humayun fifteen years of exile and the death of Sher Shah to regain control over his lost city once again. He undertook the task of restoring the city to its former glory. However, he was not destined to rule it for long, for barely a year later, he slipped down his library staircase and met with a tragic end.

With the shifting of the capital cities of the greatest of the Mughal emperors, Akbar and Jahangir, who were next in line of succession, to Fatehpur Sikri and Agra respectively, Delhi fell into a deep shadow once again. Akbar, who succeeded his father Humayun, lived mostly in Agra, where he lies buried, and his son, Jahangir, left just as small a mark on the great imperial city of

One of the many gates of Purana Qila

Delhi as his illustrious father had done. It declined in importance for a few decades. Resurrection would come seven decades later, with the construction of the splendid seventh city of Delhi by Shah Jahan, the son of Jahangir.

Political stability in the long Mughal era led to a new syncretic Indian culture, a combination of the traditions of different communities. Apart from other things, the Mughals brought with them the artistic traditions of Islam, and these combined with the local styles to produce art of great grandeur and variety in architecture and design. Mosques, tombs, citadels and palaces of matchless elegance and simplicity were built in Delhi. Their surfaces were often embellished with intricate carving, and calligraphy in the *nakshi* script. Planned gardens, or *charbagh*, a hallmark of the graceful Mughal style, were carefully laid out with fruit, flowering plants and shady trees around water channels, pools and fountains, and often contained graceful structures.

The rugged walls of Humayun's Purana Qila were one of the most splendid sights of the new capital city. Built in red sandstone, the fort walls - 34 metres high and 2.5 kilometres long - were arranged in an octagonal shape. Three main gates led into the fort – the Humayun Darwaza, the Talaqi Darwaza and the Bara Darwaza. The fort was surrounded by a moat fed by the River Yamuna, which then flowed past its eastern side.

A short distance away, the magnificent tomb of Humayun, unprecedented in size and proportion, was built by his wife, Hamida Banu Begum. This tomb introduced high arches and double domes to Indian architecture. The top of its dome was 42 metres high - more than half as high as the Qutb Minar! The mausoleum took eight years to build and is a fine example of early Mughal architecture in red sandstone and white marble. This striking combination was commonly seen in later Mughal monuments. This was also the first tomb to be built in the centre of a planned garden. Humayun's Tomb is known to have inspired many other grand Mughal tombs like Akbar's Tomb at Sikandra and culminated in the construction of the great Taj Mahal at Agra, which was built over eighty years later.

Painting, music, dance, craftsmanship and even cuisine attained new levels of sophistication. The exquisite Mughal miniature paintings were made in the finest detail in bright colours, and were a blend of Indian, Persian and European influences. The Mughal court language was Persian, but linguistic exchanges led to the development of Urdu, which later evolved into a literary language used to compose poetry and prose.

New forms of music developed, such as the *tarana, dadra* and ghazal. Folk music was also blended into courtly music. Tansen, one of the *navratnas* (or 'Nine Gems') of Akbar's court was regarded as the greatest musician of Mughal times. Mian Tansen invented several new ragas. Emperor Jahangir, a lover

The magnificent Humayun's Tomb

of music like his forefathers, is said to have composed many secular Hindi songs. The interaction of Hindu and Muslim styles of dancing also led to the development of Kathak into a strong dance tradition.

In matters of religion too, the liberal Akbar attempted an amalgam of beliefs of the good points of all religions – Hinduism, Islam, Jainism, Sufiism and Zoroastrianism – the *Din-i-Ilahi* or Divine Faith to promote universal love and harmony. However, it didn't have too many followers and faded into obscurity soon after his death.

Right from the beginning, Mughal women were highly educated, and the *zenana* or household held great influence over the emperors and their courts. The older matriarchs – mothers, aunts as also foster mothers, wives and sisters – wielded power and respect. Over time, as the older Timurid women passed away, they were replaced by Rajput and Persian wives who brought with them their new customs and ways.

The writings of Mughal noblewomen, such as the historical memoirs in Persian titled *Humayun-Nama* of Gulbadan Begum, the daughter of Babur and Humayun's sister, have become precious sources of information of the history of the *zenana*, the royal households and the period. Many noblewomen had enormous wealth at their disposal to invest and spend. They were given allowances from the royal treasury, as also grants of land, the yield of which became theirs. Several like Jahangir's mother, Mariam-uz-Zamani, his wife, Begum Nur Jahan, and Shah Jahan's daughter, Princess Jahanara, who was bestowed with the title of *Padshah Begum* or First Lady by her father, owned properties and had their own trade. Jahanara owned a large fleet of ships, which she used for extensive foreign trade and *haj* pilgrimages. Moreover, expensive gifts by kings, courtiers and merchants were commonly given to the noblewomen on various occasions.

Today, the River Yamuna has changed its course, but the splendid citadel of the Purana Qila stands in the heart of today's metropolis, forming an effective backdrop to the 215-acre Delhi National Zoological Park.

Barely 2 kilometres away, the first of the great Mughal architectural masterpieces, the stunning Humayun's Tomb, stands adjacent to the Nizamuddin East locality. It is a mandatory stop for tourists in New Delhi. The tomb was designated a UNESCO World Heritage site in 1993 and its magnificence was restored by the Aga Khan Trust for Culture in partnership with the ASI, over a period of six years.

A beautiful example of Mughal calligraphy

The placid waters of the Purana Qila Lake are popular with tourists who enjoy the pedal boats and water scooters here, just off the busy Mathura Road. It's next to the vast Pragati Maidan exhibition ground, a central venue for large fairs, exhibitions and conventions. A spectacular sound-and-light show, organized by Delhi Tourism at the ancient Purana Qila fort every evening, brings to life the fascinating story of Delhi.

Exploits of the Early Mughals

Dazzling diamonds...a lost kingdom...splendid tombs...a king who carried books to the battlefield...the Indian adventure of the early Mughals is peppered with fascinating stories of their many feats and failures, making their vibrant history come alive.

Babur the 'Tiger'

Babur means 'tiger'. According to legend, Babur, the founder of the great Mughal dynasty, was fearless in battle, a fine fencer, a good archer and a superb horseman. He was so strong and physically fit that he would carry two men, one on each shoulder, and walk uphill and run downhill, simply to keep himself fit. It is also said that he would swim across every major river he encountered, including the River Ganga, which he said he swam across twice!

> 'I swam across the River Ganges for amusement. I counted my strokes and found that I swam over in thirty-three strokes. I then took a breath and swam back to the other side... '
>
> – From Babur's lively memoir, the *Baburnama*

He was a talented poet and writer, apart from his military prowess, and the *Baburnama*, written in Chagatai Turkic, forms the main source for details about his life. It was translated into

Persian during the reign of his grandson, Akbar. Babur was a descendant of both Changez and Timur, although he took greater pride in his Timurid lineage, and considered himself a Timurid and Chagatai Turkic. In fact, he is considered a national hero in Uzbekistan and Kyrgyzstan, and many of his poems are popular folk songs there.

Babur was famous for hunting lions, the descriptions of which he has mentioned in his memoirs. He also writes of encountering rhinoceroses along the banks of the River Indus. Indeed, he was a keen naturalist, and the *Baburnama* has detailed observations of the flora and fauna of his new country, India, apart from valuable impressions of his life. A great lover of gardens, he intensely missed the beautiful landscape, the fruit and flowers of his old home and tried to beautify his surroundings in the hot, arid plains of the north, in his favourite *charbagh* style, which later Mughal kings adopted in Delhi and Agra. The construction of gardens was indeed a beloved imperial pastime of the Mughals! However, despite its flat and dusty landscape, Babur admitted that this was a large, fertile country 'with lots of gold and money'.

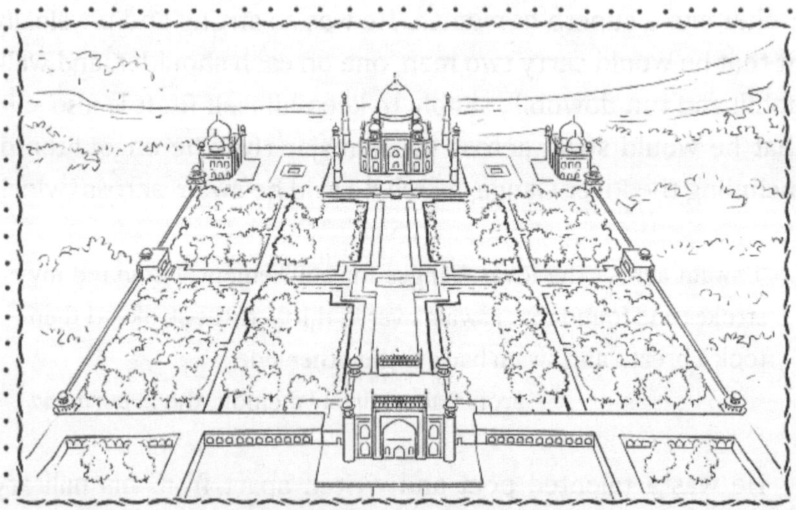

A typical Mughal *charbagh* design

Babur's preoccupation with wars and military campaigns prevented him from consolidating his gains in the Indian subcontinent. His campaigns in the north-west resulted in 'towers of skulls', and the plunder of villages and towns by his army. The instability of the new Mughal Empire became evident later under his son, Humayun, who was driven into exile in Persia by rebels.

In 1530, when his beloved Humayun became deathly ill, Babur is said to have offered his life to God in exchange for Humayun's, walking seven times around his bed to complete the vow. Humayun recovered and Babur's health declined. He died the same year in Agra. He had reigned in India for only four years.

'Mountain of Light': The Dazzling Kohinoor

The victorious Babur quickly took possession of Delhi and Agra after the First Battle of Panipat in 1526, when Sultan Ibrahim Lodi was slain and his vast army routed. Losing no time, he ordered his son Humayun to ride to Agra, the capital of the Lodi sultans the very same day, to protect its treasures and resources from looting. He had heard that the Agra Fort housed immense treasures, which included a diamond that defied description.

The terrified family of the Raja of Gwalior, who had been killed at Panipat, was captured by the Mughal army while trying to escape from the Agra Fort. Humayun guaranteed them their safety and, in return, they gratefully gave him a mass of precious stones, including their most valuable jewel – an enormous diamond, believed to be later called the Kohinoor, or 'Mountain of Light'.

Meanwhile, Babur celebrated his arrival in Delhi three days after his victory at Panipat, with a festival on the banks of the River Yamuna. After his prayers, he marched onwards to Agra where Humayun presented him with the magnificent diamond.

Enraptured by the enormous precious gem, Babur called it the 'Diamond of Babur' and even mentioned it in the *Baburnama* as weighing just over 187 old carats – approximately the size of the 186-carat Kohinoor. He commented that the jewel was so valuable that it could 'provide food for the entire world for two and a half days'!

The Kohinoor is not known to have ever been bought or sold. Reportedly mined in Kollur on the southern banks of the River Krishna, this magnificent gem was indeed the largest known diamond in the world, coveted by various Hindu, Mughal, Persian, Afghan, Sikh and British rulers who fought bitterly over it through different times in different lands. It always changed hands as a result of conquests, passing from one conqueror to another as a symbol of power and grandeur. The Kohinoor is traditionally supposed to bring good luck to the woman who wears it, but bears the curse of ill-luck for a man. And, indeed, the Kohinoor had a chequered history.

After Babur's death, the precious gem was inherited by his son, Humayun, from whom it passed on to successive generations of Mughal rulers, including Shah Jahan, who set the matchless diamond in his legendary Peacock Throne. This was the seat of Mughal emperors in India, and was placed in the Diwan-i-Khas in the Red Fort of Delhi. Years later, this throne was carried away over the Hindukush mountains towards Nadir Shah's kingdom in Persia after he had plundered the capital city of Delhi.

The Kohinoor came back into the possession of the Sikh rulers of Punjab when Ranjit Singh acquired it from the descendants of Ahmad Shah Abdali. After Punjab was annexed by the British in 1849, Ranjit Singh's youngest son, Duleep Singh, only ten years of age, was made to renounce all claims of sovereignty, and 'presented' the diamond to Queen Victoria. It was re-cut to

The Kohinoor diamond in the British crown

enhance its brilliance and conform to contemporary European tastes. So the enormous stone of 186 carats was now reduced to a shallow oval of 105.5 carats.

One of the largest diamonds in human history as also one of the largest cut-diamonds in the world today, the Kohinoor is mounted in the centre of Britain's late Queen Mother's crown. As part of the famed British Crown Jewels, it is on public display in the Jewel House at the Tower of London, where it is viewed by millions of visitors each year.

In recent years, there have been several demands for the return of the Kohinoor to India. In fact, governments in Iran, Afghanistan, Pakistan and India have all laid claim to this dazzling 'Mountain of Light'.

The Love of Humayun's Life

The second Mughal emperor, Humayun, or 'the fortunate one', was on the run. He had lost the kingdom his father, Babur, had established in India and, along with his half-brother, Hindal Mirza, he took refuge in Sind with the Sultan of Thatta, Shah Hussain.

They had spent many days travelling through a perilous and bleak desert, and now finally found some rest. Humayun's stepmother, Dildar Banu, who was Hindal's mother, gave a banquet in his honour, and among the guests she invited was the beautiful Hamida Banu who was only fourteen years old. Humayun instantly fell in love with the lively girl.

Hamida Banu Begum

Hamida's father, a Persian Sufi, popularly known as Mir Baba Dost, was Hindal's spiritual instructor, and there was a close bond between the two families. However, the feisty Hamida was very reluctant to marry the dethroned emperor. In fact, she insisted that she neither wanted an autocratic husband nor wished to be part of any royal harem. Also, Humayun was almost twenty years older than her!

'I shall marry...a man whose collar my hand can touch and not one whose skirt it does not reach!' she is said to have observed to Dildar Banu.

After resisting the proposal for forty days, Hamida Banu finally gave in and agreed to marry the emperor-in-exile. In the fifteen years that she would be married to Humayun, she never once left his side despite the hard conditions they had to endure in exile.

Akbar's mother, Hamida Banu Begum, had her own lavishly illustrated copy of the *Ramayana*, translated into Persian at Akbar's directive. It had over 450 folios and 56 large illustrations, and opened with an illuminated rosette and delicate gold figures and flowers, along with the first lines of text. It remained with her till her passing. She had special interest in the epic, and is said to have related to the hardship and endurance shown by Sita. It is now one of the treasures of Doha's Museum of Islamic Art, and testifies to medieval India's rich cross-culture.

A year later, in 1542, while still on the run, a son was born to them in Umerkot, where they had taken refuge with the Rajput king, Rana Prashad. The baby boy was named in accordance with a dream that Humayun had had after his defeat in Kannauj, when he was heading for Lahore. While in a state of utter dejection, he had dreamt of a holy man in green clothes who held a staff and said, 'Be joyful, do not despair'.

He then handed his staff to Humayun, saying, 'The Almighty will give you a son, whose name will be Jalaluddin Mohammad Akbar.'

Humayun regained the throne of Delhi after a long exile, but 'the fortunate one' was not destined to rule for long. He died barely a year later, and the thirteen-year-old Akbar ascended the throne.

The new Mughal emperor often sought his mother's advice, recognizing her shrewd intelligence. Hamida outlived Humayun by fifty years and is remembered for building Humayun's tomb under the patronage of her son, Akbar the Great.

Humayun's Favourite Retreat

Humayun was a great book lover. His fondness for books went so far that he would carry a selection of works even when he was engaged on the battlefield! During his expeditions to Bengal and Gujarat, he carried many of his favourite manuscripts with him.

It was eleven months since he had reclaimed his kingdom from Sher Shah Suri. On his way from Lahore to Agra, Humayun's royal entourage and army had halted at Din Panah, the sixth city of Delhi, which he had established twenty-three years before.

Here, Humayun's personal library and observatory, the Sher Mandal, was his favourite retreat. It was a two-storey octagonal pavilion in red sandstone, located within the Purana Qila at its highest point. Steep steps led to the roof of the Sher Mandal, which offered a panoramic view of the city. An octagonal *chhatri* supported by eight pillars and decorated with white marble stood on its roof. Humayun would often relax in his library with a pipeful of opium, surrounded by his beloved books. His valuable manuscripts were kept in safe custody here. Here too, Mir Sayyid Ali, a leading Persian miniature artist, taught drawing to the young Akbar. In fact, both Humayun and Akbar took lessons in drawing, following what is now known as the Mughal school of art.

It was a sunny winter afternoon. Humayun was on the rooftop of his library, having called astrologers here to discuss plans for setting up a centre to study the movement of the celestial bodies.

Self-portrait of Mir Sayyid Ali, a master miniature artist of Mughal times

Sher Mandal - Humayun's favourite retreat

As the sun sank low in the horizon, he was descending the library staircase with an armful of books, when he heard the muezzin's call to prayer. As always, he bowed his head in deep reverence. However, his foot got entangled in his robe and he tumbled down the flight of stairs, hitting his head on a rugged stone. Three days later, Humayun died. He was succeeded by his young son, the thirteen-year-old Akbar.

With the death of Humayun, the story of the great city he hoped to create also came to a tragic end. The site, which witnessed the rise and fall of two dominant empires - Mughal and Sur - now lies in ruins in the Purana Qila. Humayun's library, the Sher Mandal, is the only surviving palace structure within the fort and has become a notable tourist attraction. Inside it lie remnants of decorative plaster and traces of stone shelves where the emperor's books were presumably placed. However, it's no longer possible to climb up to the second floor from where he had fallen.

This group of ancient structures is flanked today by the Delhi Zoo, the Purana Qila Lake and the Bhairon Temple.

Hemu Vikramaditya: King for a Month

Hemu began life as a vegetable seller on the streets of Rewari, south-west of Delhi, in present-day Haryana - but destiny had other plans for him! Rewari lay on the main trade route to the capital from Persia and Mesopotamia, and he began sending supplies for Sher Shah Suri's army. Sher Shah's son and successor, Islam Shah, recognized Hemu's intelligence and administrative skills, and appointed him as his market superintendent. He went on to make him his personal adviser in not just trade and commerce, but also politics. Hemu soon rose to become chief of intelligence, and governor of Delhi and Punjab.

It was a turbulent period in the north of the country, for the Afghans and Mughals constantly fought for power. Hemu now served as the general and *wazir* of the last of the Sur kings, Adil Shah Suri, having proved his loyalty, capability and military skills. He subdued the many Afghan rebels on the one hand and fought the Mughal forces of Humayun on the other, winning as many as twenty-two battles for the ruler without a single defeat!

With the death of Humayun in January 1556, Hemu's forces occupied Agra and marched towards Delhi, greatly alarming its Mughal commander, Tardi Beg Khan, who demanded huge reinforcements from the child-emperor, Akbar, and his regent Bairam Khan.

Hemu's forces included 1,000 war elephants, 50,000 cavalry, fifty-one cannons and 500 light cannons.

The fierce Battle of Delhi was fought in October 1556 at Tughlakabad. As many as 3,000 Mughal forces were killed in a day as Tardi Beg fled. Hemu captured Delhi and appointed himself ruler in place of Adil Shah. He was crowned with religious rites at the Purana Qila under the title of Samrat Hemchandra Vikramaditya, in the presence of Afghan and Rajput commanders. It was a title adopted by many Hindu emperors in the past.

The new king issued coins in his name, reorganized the army and also made reforms in trade and commerce, removing corrupt officers. It was a unique interlude after 350 years of Muslim rule in the history of Delhi. But not for long!

Hemu is crowned king at the Purana Qila

The Mughals had started marshalling their troops anew with the aim to to recapture Delhi. Tardi Beg was executed by Bairam Khan for his cowardice. Barely a month later, Mughal forces marched towards Delhi under Bairam Khan. They met Hemu's army at the historic battlefield of Panipat where, thirty years earlier, Akbar's grandfather, Babur, had defeated Ibrahim Lodi in the First Battle of Panipat. Thirteen-year-old Akbar was stationed at a safe distance from the battle lines, guarded by 5,000 well-trained troops. Hemu headed his forces of 1,500 war elephants, and 30,000 trained Rajput and Afghan horsemen. It seemed victory would be Hemu's in this fiercely fought Second Battle of Panipat, when a stray arrow pierced his eye. As he dropped unconscious, his army fell into disarray and was defeated in the confusion. The injured Hemu was captured, and beheaded by Akbar, who took the title of Ghazi, a tribute of honour for a warrior.

And so, the dreams of the valiant Hemu came to nought in November 1556, barely a month after he had been crowned king of Delhi. His supporters erected a memorial for him at the location where he was executed in Panipat, now known as Hemu's Samadhi Sthal.

The Magical Couplets of Abdur Rahim

Who is not familiar with the reflective *dohas* (couplets) of Rahim? Written for every occasion in life in the Braj dialect, school students study him along with the famous trinity of medieval Bhakti poets, Surdas, Tulsidas and Kabir. Here are some everlasting gems:

Samay paay phal hot hai, samay paay jhari jaat,
Sadaa rahe nahin ek si, kaa Rahim pachhitaat.

(Fruit ripens and then withers according to its own season. Times change, so we should not worry about bad times lasting forever, says Rahim.)

Gahi sarnagati Ram ki, bhavsagar ki naav
Rahiman jagat udhar ko, aur na kachhu upay.

(The only way to achieve salvation is through unconditional surrender to Ram, the all-pervading consciousness. Surrender is the boat that will sail you through the ocean of worldly life. Here Rahim uses Hindu references despite being a Muslim.)

He was also said to be an ardent devotee of the Hindu god, Krishna, to whom he dedicated many of his *dohas* and poems. These are all eloquent expressions of a mingling of cultures.

Not just a poet, Abdur Rahim was a proficient soldier and statesman as well. One of the *navratnas* in the court of Akbar, he was the only son of Bairam Khan – Akbar's trusted uncle, guardian and regent after his father Humayun's early death.

Born in Delhi, Rahim was barely four years old when his father was assassinated in Gujarat. He was brought safely to Akbar's court with his mother and grew up into an accomplished young man under the personal care of the emperor who later gave him the title of *mirza* and made him a commander with the title of *Khan-i-Khanan* (lord of the lords).

Abdur Rahim Khan-i-Khanan

Abdur Rahim Khan-i-Khanan accompanied Akbar on his military expeditions and also became Mir Ard, the one who heard the thousands of applications addressed to the emperor. He was appointed tutor to Prince Salim (later emperor Jahangir) and one of his daughters was married to Prince Daniyal. After Akbar's death, he served under Jahangir for twenty-one years. However, his life became one of ups and downs as his two sons supported Prince Khusrau in his struggle for succession against his father Jahangir and paid for it with their lives. Rahim himself supported the unsuccessful rebellion of Prince Khurram, the future Shah Jahan, against his father. His titles were taken away in the course of these conflicts but restored in his final years.

More than his military skills, Abdur Rahim was known for the flourish of his pen. He was a gifted linguist and wrote brilliantly in Braj, Sanskrit, Arabic and Persian. He even spoke some Portuguese. He translated the *Baburnama* from Turkish to Persian. Akbar was known as a secular ruler who never discriminated on the basis of religion, and Abdur Rahim shared his beliefs. He studied the ancient Indian scriptures and astrology in depth, and compiled two books on astrology in Sanskrit. Over the years, Rahim earned enormous respect as one of the greatest Indian poets from the medieval era.

Rahim constructed a grand mausoleum for his beloved wife, Mah Banu Begum, in Delhi in 1598, with a marble and red sandstone façade. It was the first Mughal tomb built for a woman, five decades before the construction of the Taj Mahal. It also became his final resting place almost thirty years later. Rahim's tomb stands prominently on the busy Mathura Road, in the neighbourhood of Nizamuddin East, close to the *dargah* of Nizamuddin Auliya as also Humayun's Tomb.

After six years of intensive work, the tomb now has beautiful *charbagh* gardens, re-laid stone pathways and illuminated arches. It has often been compared to the Taj Mahal, for both were built as enduring symbols of love.

Timeline:
1628–1707 CE

9

The Seventh City
The Splendour of Shahjahanabad

A Paradise on Earth

If there be heaven on earth,
It is this, it is this, it is this!

– Persian couplet by Amir Khusro,
inscribed at Red Fort's Diwan-i-Khas

It was Akbar's grandson, the magnificent builder, Shah Jahan, or 'King of the World', who restored the grandeur of the old city. He transferred his capital from Agra back to Delhi in 1639 and laid the foundations of the seventh city of Delhi.

This was an entirely new city called Shahjahanabad. Interestingly, the architectural rules laid down in the ancient Hindu text, the *Vastu Shastra*, played an important role in the layout. The whole city was protected by a wall and fourteen imposing gateways to the city were built. These were always heavily guarded and kept locked at night to keep the citizens of the new capital city safe.

The Red Fort or Lal Qila was Shah Jahan's magnificent red sandstone citadel, laid along the right bank of the River Yamuna as an irregular octagon. Its massive 2.5-kilometre-long wall of red sandstone stands 23 metres high and encloses a complex of grand halls, ornamented palaces, projecting balconies and gardens. Indeed, some of the finest examples of later Mughal architecture are found within the Red Fort, which served as the home of Mughal emperors for about 200 years.

Shah Jahan, accompanied by his three sons – Dara Shikoh, Shah Shuja and Aurangzeb – and their maternal grandfather, Abu'l-Hasan Asaf Khan

Shah Jahan had the legendary Peacock Throne made to celebrate his reign. It stood glittering with precious jewels – rubies, garnets, pearls and diamonds that included the fabulous Kohinoor – on a marble platform in the centre of the *Diwan-i-am*, or Hall of Public Audience. The smaller *Diwan-i-Khas* or Hall of Private Audience had a pavilion built entirely of white marble. The magnificence and extravagance of the Delhi court was breathtaking indeed!

Standing in front of the Lal Qila, the imperial residence, Chandni Chowk or the 'moonlit square' was a bazaar with maze-like streets, its rows of shops stretching over a kilometre up to Fatehpuri Masjid, laden with goods from all corners of the empire and even other countries. A large, tree-lined canal, flowing down

A vintage painting of Chandni Chowk

its centre, led right into the walled city, reflecting the moonlight. This bustling bazaar with an opulent caravanserai, an inn for wealthy merchants, a *hammam* or communal bathhouse, and elaborate gardens, was designed by Jahanara, the powerful eldest daughter of Shah Jahan.

Here was a place where the rich could buy ornaments of precious gems, gold and silver, and *íttar* or oil-based perfumes. Persian carpets, quilts, pashmina shawls, *zari* and brocade work, dry fruit and exotic spices were all sold here to royal households and the nobility. There were also kebabs, glass hookahs and jasmine garlands. Traders from Arabia, Yemen, Syria, Turkey and Iraq too came here to sell camels, horses and weapons, while Chinese merchants arrived with eyeglasses. The bazaar was the biggest in Shahjahanabad, and a spectacle to behold!

Architecture is said to have reached a new level of elegance with the construction in 1656 of the imposing Jama Masjid in the vicinity, India's largest mosque, which is considered a marvel of Mughal and Persian architecture. This mosque blended red

Jama Masjid

sandstone and white marble harmoniously in its structure, with onion-shaped domes, elegant arches and slender minarets. It stood opposite the Red Fort and was built from materials procured from the deserted cities of Firozabad and Sher Shah's Purana Qila. The mosque was covered with intricate carvings and had verses inscribed from the holy Quran. Jama Masjid was one of the last mosques to be built by Shah Jahan, over a period of fourteen years, by more than 5,000 artisans.

Shahjahanabad was a city of many dimensions where businessmen and nobility were invited to settle. Shah Jahan permitted the building of a temporary structure to house a Jain temple in the Chandni Chowk area. Shri Digambar Jain Lal Mandir, the oldest and best-known Jain temple in Delhi, was thus built, in impressive red sandstone. Popularly known as Lal Mandir, it stood directly across from the Red Fort, and became a centre of pilgrimage for the Jain community with its three shrines dedicated to Lord Adinath, Lord Parshvanath and Lord Mahavira, the first, twenty-third and twenty-fourth and last *tirthankar* or spiritual saviour.

The Digambar sadhus, meaning 'sky-clad', are one of the two sects of Jainism, the other being the Svetambara sadhus, meaning 'white clad'. The Digambaras shun all possessions including clothes as necessary to attaining salvation. They also

A view of the splendid Red Fort and the Yamuna

The Lal Mandir or Shri Digambar Jain Temple is a landmark in Chandni Chowk

use a feather duster in accordance with their practice of non-violence, to clear their path of insects or any living things and to avoid trampling them.

Shah Jahan's sparkling new capital city dazzled foreign travellers with its splendour and wealth. Buildings like these had never been seen anywhere! In fact, Shah Jahan left behind an impressive legacy of structures constructed during his reign all over his empire. The most famous of these is, of course, the magnificent Taj Mahal in Agra, built in white marble, to hold the tomb of his beloved wife, Mumtaz Mahal, his constant companion through nineteen turbulent years. The Taj Mahal was in fact, the first of Shah Jahan's great architectural monuments, and ranks as one of the Seven Wonders of the World.

The period also saw the growth of the Urdu language from the local Hindi dialect spoken in and around the Mughal capital, and enriched by the vocabulary of its many different cultural groups like Central Asians, Afghans and Persians from which it adopted its Nastaliq form of writing. It blossomed into a literary language with a rich poetic tradition.

Of course, the grandeur of the Great Mughals did not last forever. Most of Shah Jahan's buildings were still being constructed during the desperate struggle for power between his four sons. Aurangzeb easily outclassed his older brothers in this bid for the throne. This led to Shah Jahan's long and lonely imprisonment in the Agra Fort. Aurangzeb became the new emperor and assumed the title of *Alamgir*, or 'Conqueror of the World'.

After his grand reign of thirty years, Shah Jahan could never have imagined that his last days would be so utterly tragic.

Tended by his devoted daughter Jahanara, he was confined to the Agra Fort for eight long years. According to legend, the dying Shah Jahan kept his eyes transfixed on the Taj Mahal, which was clearly visible from his place of confinement. After his death, he was buried there, beside his beloved queen.

The last powerful Mughal emperor, Aurangzeb reigned for almost fifty years, of which his capital remained in Shahjahanabad for half that period. Initially, many of the courtly traditions at Shahjahanabad were unchanged, including some Hindu traditions like the emperor's daily darshan at the Red Fort *jharokha* or balcony window, or weighing him against gold on special occasions. Later, he greatly expanded the territory of the Mughal Empire and was constantly at war in the Deccan, so his capital became a moveable one, shifting to wherever he pitched camp.

It is believed that, haunted by the blood he had spilled to gain the throne, he craved to be viewed as a just and devout ruler. He memorized the Quran, became vegetarian, and abstained from alcohol and opium.

However, it wasn't all 'heaven on earth'. An orthodox Muslim, in 1675, he publicly executed the ninth Sikh guru, Guru Tegh Bahadur. This cruel execution of the revered guru as well as several instances of brutal persecution of the Sikhs marked a turning point in Sikhism. The tenth guru, Guru Gobind Singh now actively prepared his followers to defend themselves. The frequent Mughal–Sikh skirmishes escalated into an overwhelming conflict in the later Mughal period and eroded the very foundations of Mughal power by the middle of the eighteenth century.

Having ruled most of the Indian subcontinent for nearly half a century, Aurangzeb was the second longest-reigning Mughal emperor after Akbar. Yet he had undone much of the work of his brilliant predecessors – and sadly, the rot soon set in.

It was during this dark period of history that Raja Jai Singh II of Jaipur who acknowledged the Delhi emperor's sovereignty, built his ingenious observatories in Delhi, Jaipur, Ujjain, Varanasi and

Jantar Mantar, one of the earliest astronomical observatories in the world

Mathura. The Jantar Mantar, which literally means 'calculation instruments', stands in the heart of New Delhi at Rajiv Chowk. It is an astronomical observatory with a collection of architectural and astronomical instruments, named Samrat Yantra, Jai Prakash, Ram Yantra and Misra Yantra. Their ingenuity astounds even today, but the tall buildings surrounding it make accurate observations difficult now. The Jantar Mantar complex is a popular tourist attraction of the metropolis. It has also been used as a site for protests and agitations in the capital.

Shahjahanabad is today's walled city of Old Delhi. Several of the fourteen imposing gates to this city, all built during Shah Jahan's reign – the Kashmiri Gate, the Delhi Gate, the Ajmeri Gate and the Turkman Gate, still stand. Old Delhi is densely populated with a unique old-world charm of its own. Many of its historic alleys and grand old havelis with beautifully carved doorways take visitors back in time, into an old-fashioned world of grace and refinement for which Delhi was well known!

Many of these havelis were once the residences of the city's rich and famous. Begum Samru Ki Haveli, belonging to the dancer

Begum Samru, once had nine grand fountains amidst gardens, open-air terraces, winding staircases, and Mughal, Greek and Roman architectural influences. Zeenat Mahal, named after the third and most favourite wife of Bahadur Shah Zafar, was an exquisitely adorned palace spread over four acres, with fountains, cellars and arched ceilings. These long-forgotten havelis sadly lie in a state of total neglect today, and are hardly visible with encroachments, potholes and overhanging wires everywhere!

Today Chandni Chowk is a congested bazaar, where each bylane leads into a wondrous world of silver, jewellery, spices, utensils, textiles and perfumes, among hundreds of other wares. Dariba and Kinari Bazaar have been gold and silver trading hubs since the time of Shah Jahan, and even now, jewellery shops abound here. Many handicrafts like pottery, engraving, embroidery, metal work, ivory and woodcarving originated in Shahjahanabad and still survive today, handed down the generations.

The many culinary surprises of Chandni Chowk make it a favourite with foodies as well, and its Paranthe Wali Gali and Ghantewala Halwai are legendary eateries, well over a century old! With mouthwatering *rabri*, *kulfi* and *falooda*, *jalebi*, *aloo tikki* and *poori*, *chaat* and *dahi bhalla*...it is a popular hub for local cuisine! Ballimaran is popular for its meat *nihari* while the area around Jama Masjid has plenty of eateries.

Tandoori chicken, dal *makhani* and paneer *makhani* all originated in Delhi as did butter chicken, traditionally known as *murgh makhani*, a chicken curry cooked in spiced tomatoes, butter and cream.

Several historic places of worship – the Sri Digambar Jain Lal Mandir, the Sis Ganj Gurdwara, the ancient Gauri Shankar Temple, the Central Baptist Church and the Jama Masjid still stand today in the bustling Chandni Chowk area. The vast courtyard of Jama Masjid can hold 25,000 devotees who offer *namaz*, especially during festivals.

The Jain temple is popular for its striking architecture, beautiful carvings, pure gold artwork and frescos. It is famous in the city because of the massive charity hospital for birds, called the Birds Hospital, behind the main temple complex. This unique hospital treats birds rescued from accidents and bird hawkers. After plenty of loving care, the birds are set free from the roof. It's a hospital like no other!

Of late, Chandni Chowk has been getting a greatly needed makeover, although there have been huge challenges all around, with potholes and overhanging wires, unending crowds, deafening traffic and congested inside lanes. Its main thoroughfare is now vehicle-free during the day and has been paved with red sandstone and granite from the Red Fort area to Fatehpuri Masjid, a nearly 1.4-kilometre stretch. Beautification of the area around the Jama Masjid is now underway, in the style of the mosque. A mega, multi-level parking is being constructed at Dangal Maidan. The wild tangle of overhead wires has been placed underground, and LED lighting, trees, plants, public toilets, benches and a paved footpath have replaced the earlier clutter. New signboards identify the lanes, making navigation easier.

There are also plans to renovate the iconic Town Hall, which once housed government offices, a library and a European club. This location is called the Ghantaghar after a clock tower that once stood here. It is still surrounded by Mughal-style gardens with an octagonal pool of fountains, a reminder that this land once belonged to Princess Jahanara. A long alleyway leads up to the Old Delhi Railway Station.

The historic Red Fort complex is a UNESCO World Heritage site today. The nation's focus shifts here every year on Independence Day, when the prime minister of India hoists the Indian Tricolour and addresses the nations from its ramparts. This tradition has become an integral part of the celebrations.

Sunshine and Shadow

The splendid Shahjahanabad had its place in the sun as Mughal power reached its zenith. The Mughal Empire was indeed one of the wealthiest in the entire world. However, the sun began to set for the Mughals with the tyranny of Aurangzeb's long reign, and eventually, the once-glorious Mughal dynasty fell into twilight.

The Scholar Prince and His Library

He was the favourite son of Emperor Shah Jahan and, as his eldest, was groomed to be king, but destiny had other plans for him.

Prince Dara Shikoh grew up to become a great scholar of Persian and Sanskrit, and an unorthodox Muslim. He was inclined more towards philosophy, mysticism and the fine arts, rather than military pursuits. His spiritual master was the widely respected Sufi saint of the Qadiri order, Mian Mir of Lahore, who is said to have laid the foundation stone of the Golden Temple in Amritsar at the invitation of Guru Arjun Dev. In fact, Dara Shikoh also formed a friendship with Guru Har Rai, the seventh Sikh guru.

The scholar prince sought to reconcile Hindu and Islamic thought and traditions, claiming that 'One Reality and One God' was their common core principle. Towards this effort, he set up libraries in many places including Delhi. He also authored many books. His most famous one, *Majma-ul-Bahrain* (The Confluence

Dara Shikoh (left) and his spiritual teacher, Mian Mir

of the Two Seas) is a comparative study of Vedanta and Sufism. Moreover, he translated fifty Upanishads from Sanskrit into Persian under the title *Sirr-e-Akbar* (The Great Secret), so that they could be studied by Muslim scholars. It is said that he always found the time to translate and write books, even in the midst of war or his own political storms.

He built his library in Delhi in red sandstone, featuring simple Mughal architecture, to house his personal collection of books and manuscripts. This library also became a meeting space for him to interact with scholars of different religions and ideologies. He set up another library at Agra with additional enclosures for translators, painters and book binders.

Unfortunately, Dara Shikoh was defeated in a brutal battle of succession and paraded through the streets of Delhi in chains by his younger brother, Aurangzeb, while his father was still alive. He was subsequently beheaded.

The Dara Shikoh Library still stands on the campus of Ambedkar University near Kashmiri Gate. It was later renovated by the British who added Roman columns to the façade and gave it a colonial look. It now serves as a museum under the protection of the Archaeological Survey of India. It is a tragic reminder of a peace-loving and scholarly prince who could not be king.

The Death of Music

Music and ritual dance were an integral part of the devotion of the mystical Sufis to the divine. However, the austere Aurangzeb adopted a less mystical, more severe form of Islam. This was based on his own conservative interpretation of Islamic principles.

According to this, Islam did not allow music, so it is said that he banished musicians, dancers and singers from the Delhi court during his time. Kathak dancers returned to their rural homes and villages and went into hiding. They were treated as social outcasts. He also stopped the production of artwork, including the delicate Mughal miniature painting that had reached its height of perfection before his rule.

The emperor passed stern orders that, if his officials heard the sound of singing and musical instruments in any house or elsewhere, they were to hasten there and arrest as many as they could and break all the instruments!

Aurangzeb

This led to the destruction of a lot of musical instruments, and naturally created much unhappiness everywhere. Court musicians who had been part of the profession for generations suddenly found themselves unemployed. They planned to appease the emperor with an unusual plan. One Friday, when Aurangzeb was to go to Moti Masjid in the Red Fort for prayers, about a thousand of them organized a funeral procession of their instruments. Hearing their loud lamentation, the emperor enquired about the reason for their grief.

He was told that, as the orders of the emperor had killed music, they were, therefore, taking her to the grave. Aurangzeb calmly retorted that they should pray for the soul of music, '... and bury music so deep under the earth that no sound or echo of it may rise again.' Thus, the Mughal court, which under Shah Jahan had been the grand centre of patronage for the arts, ceased to be so during Aurangzeb's reign. It became austere and desolate. However, despite his orders, music continued to flourish in private as the royal family, the nobility and the courtiers were not prepared to live without it. When Aurangzeb's court shifted to the Deccan in the latter half of his reign, Delhi once again became a centre of music and the arts.

There is another popular legend of the time about the ban on music, relating to the Digambar Jain Lal Mandir, standing directly across from the Red Fort. The sound of its many musical instruments and beating of nagara drums disturbed the emperor, Aurangzeb, who ordered that all music here be stopped. Yet, he continued to hear musical sounds from the Lal Mandir. When officials went to check the Jain temple, they found the instruments playing melodiously by themselves. The baffled Aurangzeb is said to have visited the temple himself, and to have subsequently lifted his ban.

In his personal life too, Aurangzeb was more austere and pious than any of his predecessors. He prayed regularly and abstained from all forms of alcohol and opium. Despite all the pomp and splendour of the Mughal Empire and its unparalleled wealth, the last of the great Mughals chose to be utterly simple. He wore very plain and inexpensive clothes and few ornaments. In his later years, it is said that he even sewed prayer caps and copied the Quran by hand in his free time, to pay for his meals.

Healing Touch at Gurdwara Bangla Sahib

Gurdwara Bangla Sahib was originally a magnificent palace belonging to Raja Jai Singh of Amber (Jaipur), who was one of Aurangzeb's most important military leaders and a trusted member of his court. It was known as Jaisinghpura Palace, located in the forested village area of Jaisinghpura. Later on, it came to be known as the *bangla* or residence of the raja who converted it into a gurdwara.

Guru Har Krishan, the eighth Sikh guru, stayed here for a few months as the raja's guest in Delhi in 1664. Learning that the young Har Krishan, who was only five years old, had been appointed the spiritual head of the Sikhs, his elder brother, the thirteen-year-old Ram Rai, tried in vain to influence the leading Sikhs of Delhi and the Punjab to support him instead. Later, he even approached Emperor Aurangzeb, who had befriended him, to help him acquire the *gurugaddi*, or seat of the guru. Consequently, Aurangzeb agreed to summon Guru Har Krishan to Delhi.

Fortunately, both Raja Jai Singh and his son Raja Ram Singh were in Delhi at that time. When the Sikhs approached them for help, the Rajput chief took over the responsibility of persuading Guru Har Krishan to come to Delhi. He also gained assurance from Aurangzeb that, as long as the emperor was not satisfied about the issue of succession, the guru could stay with Raja Jai Singh and his son in his bungalow as their honoured guest.

It was at this time that a terrible epidemic of smallpox and cholera swept through the city of Delhi. Instead of resting in

Guru Har Krishan (centre)

the comfort and safety of the palatial bungalow, the young Guru Har Krishan helped the suffering with great devotion, going out to give them medicine, food and fresh water from the well of this house. Thousands are said to have recovered. He would often sit with his feet dipped in the water, hence the well came to be known as having healing powers. Since the guru helped everyone, including the local Muslim population suffering from the epidemic, they called him '*Bal Pir*', which means child saint. However, he himself contracted smallpox and eventually died. The guru was only eight years old.

After his death, Raja Jai Singh converted his fabulous mansion into a gurdwara in memory of the revered guru. It came to be called Gurdwara Bangla Sahib. Raja Jai Singh also built a tank over the well. Its water was revered as having healing properties and was known as *amrit* or nectar.

Over the years, the structure of the original gurdwara underwent several changes. It was rebuilt by Sardar Bhagel Singh, an important Sikh military general, in 1783. He also supervised the construction of nine Sikh shrines in Delhi the same year, during the reign of the Mughal Emperor Shah Alam II.

Almost a century and a half later, the village of Jaisinghpura would be evacuated and demolished to make way for the modern Connaught Place shopping district of New Delhi. Interestingly, until then, the entire area was covered by forests and used as the hunting grounds for shooting partridges, along with a cluster of three villages, Raja ka Bazaar, Madhoganj and Jaisinghpura, where Gurdwara Bangla Sahib stood.

The present structure of the gurdwara was built mostly after 1947. Today, situated in the heart of New Delhi's bustling Connaught Place area, which was renamed Rajiv Chowk in 2013 after former prime minister Rajiv Gandhi, the gurdwara and its large water tank or *sarovar*, have been constructed entirely with donations and the *karseva* or voluntary labour of devotees. Its holy water is revered for its healing properties and is carried home by Sikhs throughout the world.

Dedicated to the eighth Sikh guru, Gurdwara Bangla Sahib is Delhi's most prominent gurdwara, instantly recognizable by its magnificent golden dome. Built in white marble, it has enormous arches, set with beautiful inlay work. Devotional music or *gurbani* resounds throughout the complex continuously. As at all Sikh pilgrimage sites, *langar* or free food is served to all here every day. The sprawling complex also houses a school, a museum, an art gallery, a library and a hospital. It is a place of pilgrimage for thousands of Sikhs, Hindus and tourists every day, who come here to honour the memory of the child-healer, Guru Har Krishan.

The Guru's Great Sacrifice

The conflict between the Sikhs and the Mughal rulers started during the reign of Emperor Jahangir when Guru Arjun Dev, the fifth guru of the Sikhs, was tortured to death by him. This conflict only intensified during the reign of Emperor Aurangzeb.

Offered a choice between death and adoption of Islam, the the ninth Sikh guru, Guru Tegh Bahadur, chose death.

'God is one,' he said. 'Whatever name you call Him, He is the same. Our paths take us to the same destination... you can kill my body but not the spirit of my people.'

The guru and his followers were imprisoned. On 11 November 1675, Guru Tegh Bahadur was beheaded in public under a banyan tree in Chandni Chowk, close to the Red Fort, upon Aurangzeb's orders. He thus gave up his head (*sis*) but did not give up his faith.

Gurdwara Sis Ganj in Shahjahanabad marked this spot where the gurdwara was built a century later by Sardar Bhagel Singh in memory of the brave Sikh guru who had made the supreme sacrifice for freedom of worship. His martyrdom gave him the title of *Hind-di-Chadar* or 'Protector of India'.

The magnificent Sis Ganj Gurdwara is built in the then prevalent architectural style with mesh-work windows, pavilions and parapets, all in sandstone instead of the usual white marble of the other gurdwaras. It is known to have served both as a mosque and as a gurdwara, alternating itself according to the volatile political climate of the period. It became a site of prolonged dispute between the two communities, and litigation followed. Eventually, the Privy Council during the British Raj ruled in favour of the Sikh litigants. In 1930 it was finally converted into a full-fledged gurdwara with gold-gilded domes.

Located in the vicinity of the Red Fort and Jama Masjid, the Sis Ganj Gurdwara stands today in Old Delhi's main Chandni Chowk Road, right in the heart of the bustling market. Devotees flock from far and wide to this famous Sikh pilgrimage site.

Here, the trunk of the banyan tree beneath which Guru Tegh Bahadur was beheaded still stands, along with the well where he bathed while he was in prison. Also, adjoining the gurdwara, stands the *kotwali* (police station) where the guru and his disciples were imprisoned. Across the narrow road from the gurdwara stands a small shrine that marks the area where three of the guru's closest disciples were subjected to atrocities.

During the Republic Day parade, the Sikh regiment of the Indian army salutes the Sis Ganj Gurdwara after saluting the president of India. This is the only instance of a regiment of the Indian army saluting twice in the course of the Republic Day parade.

The Story of Gurdwara Rakab Ganj

It is said that after Guru Tegh Bahadur was beheaded at Chandni Chowk, Aurangzeb forbade anyone from moving his decapitated head and body. Suddenly, such a violent dust storm is said to have risen that nothing could be seen. It grew dark and started raining heavily.

Under cover of the darkness, two brave followers of the guru defied the emperor's orders. The severed head was taken by Bhai Jaita, who escaped 500 kilometres away to Anandpur Sahib in Punjab. Here it was cremated by his son, Gobind Rai, later Guru Gobind Singh, the tenth and last guru of the Sikhs.

Almost at the same time, Bhai Lakhi Shah Banjara and his son, Bhai Naghaiya, bravely took the headless body of their guru and, placing it under cotton bales in a bullock cart, escaped to their home in the old Raisina village. To avoid detection, they placed their guru's headless body on a bed, and then cremated it by burning their entire home. They placed his ashes in an urn and buried it on the spot.

This place came to be later known as Rakab Ganj, as most of its residents were employed in manufacturing stirrups, which are attached to a horse's saddles, for the cavalry of the Mughal army. Hence the name '*rakab*', which is Persian for 'stirrups'. Gurdwara Rakab Ganj stands here today. The Gurdwara has two prayer halls. The main prayer hall stands where the body of Guru Tegh Bahadur was cremated.

Guru Gobind Singh was now formally installed as the leader of the Sikhs at the tender age of nine years, becoming the tenth and last Sikh guru.

It is said that, after the martyrdom of his father, Guru Tegh Bahadur, the tenth guru declared that he would create such a *panth* or community that would challenge oppressive rulers in every walk of life, to restore justice, equality and peace for all of mankind. This was the beginning of the Khalsa, created in 1699. Guru Gobind Singh further militarized his followers after Aurangzeb killed four of his sons. He sent Aurangzeb the *Zafarnama*, or Epistle of Victory, a famous letter in 111 verses in Persian, after the Battle of Chamkaur, indicting the emperor's treachery and rebuking his weaknesses as a human being and excesses as a leader.

The Sikhs believe that this document filled Aurangzeb with remorse; he lost the will to live and it culminated in his death in 1707. He was succeeded by his son Bahadur Shah I who won his throne with the help of the Sikh army.

When Guru Gobind Singh came to Delhi in 1707 to meet Prince Muazzam, who later became the Mughal emperor, Bahadur Shah I, he discovered, with the help of the local Sikhs, the exact location of where the cremation of his father had taken place – the old Raisina village. He built a simple memorial there.

However, claiming the land for a gurdwara here was not easy. A mosque had been constructed at this very site. The Sikhs later claimed this spot as their sacred place, in memory of their guru's great sacrifice. However, the Muslims strongly objected to the dismantling of their mosque. Swords were drawn as animosity grew. However, the Sikhs offered to reconstruct the mosque for the Muslims if the urn containing the ashes of their revered guru was not found buried below.

The excavation work commenced at the site in the presence of Mughal officials. And indeed, the claim of the Sikhs proved to be correct, and they were allowed to construct Gurdwara Rakab Ganj by Emperor Shah Alam II. He granted permission to Sardar Bhagel Singh to take possession of the land for the construction of a gurdwara and garden. He also gifted them about 63 acres of land with three wells. The gurdwara was completed in 1783 at an expense of rupees 25 lakh, taking twelve years to complete.

The Sikh forces agreed to withdraw from Delhi peacefully after the construction of their religious shrines in the Mughal capital. There are ten historical gurdwaras in Delhi.

The present location of the magnificent Rakab Ganj Gurdwara is in central Delhi, near Parliament House and North Block of the Central Secretariat. Rashtrapati Bhavan, the splendid official residence of the president of India, stands in the vicinity.

The elegant gurdwara is composed mainly of white marble and is surrounded by a beautiful garden. Like most other Sikh shrines, this gurdwara has four entrances from all sides, symbolizing its accessibility to all without discrimination of caste or creed. It stands as a sacred symbol in memory of the brave Guru Tegh Bahadur who sacrificed his life for freedom of worship, and of the dedication and selflessness as portrayed by his brave followers, Bhai Lakhi Shah Banjara and his son, Bhai Naghaiya.

The Guru's Unerring Aim

It was the first visit of Guru Gobind Singh to the city of Delhi in 1707. This was in response to Prince Muazzam's urgent appeal for help in the battle of succession that followed the death of his father Aurangzeb.

Guru Gobind Singh

The guru camped with his army at a place called Mochi Bagh, a colony of cobblers. He had good feelings for the prince, the eldest son of Emperor Aurangzeb, who had refused to attack the guru in Anandpur Sahib under his father's orders. He had even been imprisoned for four months by Aurangzeb.

The guru, an accomplished archer, announced his arrival in Delhi dramatically. He shot an arrow from the camp site unerringly, into the right foot of Prince Muazzam's seat in the Red Fort, almost 12 kilometres away! The prince, who was inside the fort was greatly astonished by this display of archery and exclaimed that this must be a miracle. A second arrow followed immediately, striking the left foot of the same seat, with a small note saying that this was not a miracle but a skilled display of archery! Prince Muazzam was so impressed that he immediately accepted the supremacy of the guru. Later, the prince would ascend the throne as Emperor Bahadur Shah 1.

The name of Mochi Bagh was changed to Moti Bagh afterwards, and a gurdwara was built here to commemorate the place where Guru Gobind Singh had sent his arrows with flawless aim towards the Mughal throne. The gate of the camp from where the guru shot his arrows has been preserved along with the old building. The Guru Granth Sahib has been installed here as a mark of respect to the superb archery of the guru. The skyline of Delhi with the Red Fort can still be seen from this spot.

The magnificent Moti Bagh Gurdwara was built here later, in pure white marble. Today this historic gurdwara stands on the Ring Road in Moti Bagh, and people come here in large numbers to seek the blessings of Guru Gobind Singh who taught that 'the same God dwells in the temple and the mosque'.

Timeline:
1707–94 CE

10

The Twilight Years

❁ The Sun Sets on the City ❁

The splendid Shahjahanabad had its place in the sun as Mughal power reached its zenith. It was indeed one of the wealthiest dynasties in the entire world. However, after Aurangzeb's long reign, the glory of the Mughals began to fade.

With the fall of the mighty empire by the mid-eighteenth century, there began a many-sided struggle for mastery of the north. The feeble Mughals were defenceless against raids and skirmishes by the Marathas. At the same time, many Mughal nobles asserted their independence to found small states. The final blow was the devastation caused by Nadir Shah's invasion. It was as though darkness had gripped Delhi! The once formidable Mughal Empire was reduced to a strip of land around the capital.

It is said that as Nadir Shah, the Emperor of Persia, marched in triumph towards Delhi in 1739, a rumour spread that he was dead. The elated inhabitants of Delhi not only celebrated this but were even bold enough to attack a few Persian soldiers. The consequences for the already tottering city were disastrous.

On an order from Nadir Shah to carry out *qatl-e-aam*, or killing of the common public, his soldiers plundered Delhi and brutally massacred its citizens. The densely populated areas of Chandni Chowk, the fruit market, the Dariba bazaar and the buildings around Jama Masjid were burnt to cinders. The once magnificent capital city of Delhi was now an utterly ravaged city, strewn with corpses.

Nadir Shah

The ruling Mughal emperor, Muhammad Shah 'Rangila', was forced to beg for mercy. Nadir Shah agreed to withdraw on condition that Muhammad Shah handed over the keys of his royal treasury. And so, he did.

The royal treasury was sacked, and its contents seized. When Nadir Shah left Delhi after 57 days, he took along with him the fabulous Peacock Throne, and the priceless Kohinoor and Darya-i-Noor diamonds. It is said that his total collection of booty was worth 700 million rupees, loaded on 700 elephants, 4,000 camels and 12,000 horses. Apart from this, he also took with him 7,000 craftsmen, 100 stone-cutters and 200 carpenters. And along with them all went the last traces of Mughal pride and splendour.

Moved to sorrow and tears, Mir Taqi Mir, an eminent contemporary Urdu poet, wrote about the ghost city of Delhi –

Once through this ruined city did I pass –
I espied a lonely bird on a bough and asked
'What know you of this wilderness?'
It replied: 'I can sum it up in two words:
Alas, Alas!'

Nine years later, Delhi was ruthlessly rocked again by the invasion of the Afghans, led by Ahmad Shah Abdali, who was one of Nadir Shah's foremost generals. Abdali led as many as seven invasions into India in a period of almost twenty years, from 1748 to 1767. These repeated incursions brought the decaying Mughal Empire to the brink of collapse.

In January 1757, Ahmad Shah Abdali captured Delhi and, after raiding the city, marched on to overrun most of northern India.

Once again, the Urdu poet Mir Taqi Mir was witness to the barbaric invasions of Ahmad Shah Abdali. He lamented:

There was once a fair city,
Among cities of the world the first in fame.
It hath been ruined and laid desolate,
To that city I belong, Delhi is its name!

However, the Mughal dynasty remained in nominal control. Ahmad Shah Abdali installed a puppet Mughal emperor, Alamgir II, who paid him tribute.

The Afghan now came into direct confrontation with the Marathas who had been fighting a series of battles with the Mughal Empire for twenty-seven years in the Deccan, till the death of Aurangzeb in 1707. It had been like a game of snakes and ladders, with short and long conflicts, wins and defeats! The main reasons for their struggle had been Aurangzeb's oppression and his attempts to extinguish rising Maratha power. The courageous Marathas were eventually successful against the Mughals with their strategy of guerrilla warfare, and took over major territories of the Mughal Empire. This paved the way for Maratha expansion in the north.

The Maratha Empire fragmented into different holdings held by individual clans. Leading Maratha families like the Shindes of Gwalior and Ujjain, the Holkars of Indore and Malwa, the Bhonsles of Nagpur and the Gaekwads of Baroda formed the powerful Maratha Confederacy, under the leadership of the Peshwa or prime minister, at Poona (now Pune), from 1721 onwards. Later on, the clans would become more independent and difficult to control.

The Maratha Confederacy made inroads into Delhi during two Battles of Delhi in the eighteenth century. In the first battle in 1737, they attacked the Mughal capital, camping near Talkatora. The Mughals lost much of their army in the fierce attack and were compelled to ask regional rulers for help to push the Marathas back.

Twenty years later, 1757 was an eventful year. The Second Battle of Delhi was fought between the Marathas and Najib-ud-daula, the Afghan who had been given control of Delhi by Abdali earlier that year, in return for an annual tribute of twenty lakh rupees. Najib-ud-daulah was defeated by the Marathas after two weeks of intense fighting with heavy losses. He surrendered and was arrested. The Marathas thus became protectors of the Mughal throne in Delhi and exacted a tribute of fifty lakh rupees from Najib-ud-daulah, with a promise that he would never return to Delhi, nor threaten any Maratha fort. It was an interesting turn of events!

By 1758, the Marathas controlled most of the subcontinent – right from Rajasthan and Punjab in the north to Peshawar in present-day Pakistan, to today's West Bengal and Odisha in the east, and Thanjavur in the south. They also successfully drove back Ahmad Shah's son, Timur Shah, who had been left by his father as governor of Punjab and Kashmir, while he returned to Afghanistan loaded with loot. Timur fled to Afghanistan. The Marathas thus became the foremost power of the subcontinent.

The Marathas now occupied Delhi, but they had captured a ruined city, plundered heavily by both Nadir Shah and Ahmad Shah. Greatly pressed for funds to protect the Red Fort, they stripped the ornate roof of its Diwan-i-Khas of its silver. This was then melted and was made into coins, it is said, worth 28 lakh rupees of those days.

Never one to give up, Ahmad Shah returned once again to challenge the Maratha army in the Third Battle of Panipat in 1761. The Maratha advance in the north was halted for a while after their crushing defeat. However, they were back ten years later when they defeated the Afghans and recaptured the territory lost in the battle. A treaty between the Marathas and the Afghans gave them all lands east of the River Sutlej. The Mughal emperor, Shah Alam II, was restored to the throne of Delhi, this time under Maratha protection.

Shah Alam II

Those were turbulent times indeed for the ravaged city of Delhi as Afghans, Mughals, Marathas and Sikhs - all vied to fill the power vacuum. Ahmad Shah soon lost Punjab to the fierce Sikhs, who ultimately drove him away from the subcontinent.

The Sikhs had suffered immense persecution at the hands of various Mughal emperors. They had tortured and slain many of the Sikh gurus, their close kin and other revered figures. In the eighteenth century, the Sikhs organized themselves into a number of bands called *jathas*, and later into *misls*, under several able leaders. Their combined forces were known as the grand army, the Dal Khalsa. It was now their turn to march towards Delhi, determined to take their revenge on the Mughals.

It is said that the Sikhs invaded and plundered parts of present-day trans-Yamuna territories like Saharanpur, Meerut and Shahdara, in and around the city of Delhi nineteen times in the second half of the eighteenth century. They marked the rise of a new force to reckon with here. Sardar Baghel Singh led the Sikhs all the way to Delhi in 1783. Ultimately, they agreed to withdraw their forces after a treaty with the Mughal emperor.

Yet Delhi was not destined to die.

The fate of the feisty old city underwent a change once again, with the emergence of another new power on the scene, the British.

Battling for Delhi

It was a time of immense difficulties for the people of the ruined city of Delhi as the Mughal Empire tottered on the verge of collapse, and different powers battled to fill in the void. Fear and anxiety filled the air everywhere! The city's population had reduced to a fraction of what it once was, by the end of the eighteenth century. The plunders by marauders, whole-scale exoduses from Delhi and natural calamities had all taken their toll on the bruised and battered city.

The Sikhs Battle for Delhi

The Sikh forces had already invaded Delhi eleven times, raiding and plundering its outskirts. Suburbs like Paharganj, Shahdara, Jaisinghpura and Rakab Ganj were attacked and ransacked. These attacks were a retaliatory response to the sufferings that had been inflicted upon their spiritual leaders and the Sikh community under the Mughal rulers. The Sikhs were determined to assert their identity, and seek religious freedom and justice. Their aim was always to reach the Red Fort to hoist their flag. However, a shortage of supplies forced them to move back every time.

It was in 1783 that 40,000 Sikh soldiers marched to Delhi on horses and elephants and camped in the capital city, determined to reach the Red Fort this time. They divided themselves into three groups – 5,000 each were deployed at Majnu Ka Tilla and Ajmeri Gate, while 30,000 under Sardar Baghel Singh, Jassa Singh Ramgarhia and Jassa Singh Ahluwalia camped at a place just 3 kilometres from the Red Fort. This location came to be known as Tees Hazari ('thirty thousand').

When the Mughal emperor, Shah Alam II, heard about the imminent Sikh siege of the Red Fort, he ordered all its gates to be shut without delay, especially where rations were stored. When the Sikh forces ran out of food, they would be forced to retreat, he reasoned.

There was a secret of the old city waiting to be discovered! A mason from a neighbouring village disclosed to some Sikh soldiers that a part of the wall of the Red Fort had caved in, although the exterior was undamaged. This could well be their surprise access into the Red Fort! He helped them to identify this spot. Logs of wood were rammed into the weak wall, and the Sikhs entered through the opening. This place came to be known later as Mori Gate ('*mori*' in Hindi indicates a hole-like space).

It was in great triumph that the Sikhs entered the Red Fort and hoisted their flag. They even occupied the Diwan-e-Aam. Sardar Baghel Singh and his forces celebrated their great victory in Delhi by distributing sweets to the poor from a bridge close by, which later came to be called Mithai Pul (yes, '*mithai*' means 'sweets').

Emperor Shah Alam II was forced to accept the Sikh capture of the Red Fort, and offered them a treaty where he agreed to their terms. In place of vacating the Red Fort, he allowed Sardar Baghel Singh to stay on in Delhi to identify all the sites sacred to the Sikhs here, and build gurdwaras at these sites. Ten gurdwaras would be constructed in all, including Gurdwara Sis Ganj Sahib where Guru Tegh Bahadur had been executed by Mughal Emperor Aurangzeb, Gurdwara Rakab Ganj and Gurdwara Bangla Sahib.

The Sikhs were also presented 3 lakh rupees. Four thousand men stayed behind with Sardar Baghel Singh to oversee the

Sardar Baghel Singh and the Sikhs capture the Red Fort

construction of their gurdwaras. The rest of the forces left the following day, after the settlement.

Interestingly, Sardar Jassa Singh Ramgarhia carried back with him the black Stone Throne of Aurangzeb, on which he had sat and ordered the beheading of their ninth guru, Guru Tegh Bahadur. It was duly chained and tied with ropes, like a prisoner and war trophy, and taken all the way to the Golden Temple in Amritsar by elephants! Here it was presented before the Guru – the Guru Granth Sahib or Holy Book, which all Sikhs had been directed by the last Sikh Guru, Guru Gobind Singh, to accept as the Guru after him. The Stone Throne remains within the premises of the sacred shrine to this very day, in a structure called the Ramgarhia Bunga, imprisoned by railings!

Today, Tees Hazari in north Delhi is a name familiar to all Delhiwallahs as the location of the principal district court complex in Delhi. The congested bridge, Mithai Pul, still stands, a little distance away. And Mori Gate Bus Terminal is a name all bus commuters in Delhi recognize, being situated close to the present Inter State Bus Terminal (ISBT) in Kashmiri Gate.

So the names of places in Delhi which we take so much for granted today have the most incredible stories behind them!

A Lucky Escape

It was perhaps the bloodiest battle in our history. The Third Battle of Panipat, fought between the forces of Ahmad Shah Abdali and the Marathas in 1761, left about one lakh dead in one day alone. It came to be known as the 'blackest day' in India's history.

Mahadji Shinde was an important commander in the Maratha camp and a trusted lieutenant of the Peshwa, the leader of the Maratha Confederacy. He had fought most heroically at Panipat, but tactical mistakes had cost the Marathas a disastrous defeat at the hands of the Afghans. What's more, accompanying the Maratha army were over 2 lakh civilians! Many were pilgrims intent on visiting holy Hindu shrines in the north. They became sitting ducks before the Afghan forces and were slaughtered mercilessly. The Maratha army had to protect them as well as fight a war. It is said that over 60,000 civilians were killed out of a total of a lakh Maratha deaths. It was a massacre.

A whole generation of Maratha leaders lay dead on the battlefield of Panipat. The commander-in-chief of the Maratha army, Sadashivrao Bhau was killed in the battle as was Vishwasrao,

The Third Battle of Panipat was fought between the Afghans and the Marathas

the son and heir of the Peshwa, Balaji Bajirao. Mahadji Shinde was seriously injured and practically unconscious. He lay covered in blood amidst a heap of bodies, when a Pathan water carrier called Rane Khan found him. Little knowing who he was, he carried the Maratha commander away in his water-carrying leather skin, and nursed him back to health.

Mahadji spent many months recovering from his injuries, but a serious leg wound left him with a limp for the rest of his life. His survival was crucial to the revival of Maratha power in the coming years.

Mahadji never forgot his plucky rescuer on the battlefield, and indeed, for the rest of his life always kept Rane Khan by his side, declaring him to be his brother. He called him 'Bhai' and appointed him to a responsible position in his army. Later, he became his military commander with the title of Sardar Rane Khan Bhai Khawasiwale.

Eventually, a period of Maratha resurrection set in, led by Peshwa Madhavrao and completed by Mahadji. They rebuilt Maratha control in north India with a powerful army, and within ten years they had avenged the humiliating defeat at Panipat, recapturing many of their lost territories.

Mahadji Shinde

The Marathas captured Delhi once again in 1771 under the able command of Mahadji, who defeated the commander of the Red Fort. He personally brought back the Mughal emperor, Shah Alam II, from his exile in the fort of Allahabad to Delhi, where he was given back the Red Fort with a treaty. Mahadji became the regent of the Mughal Empire, reducing the Mughals to puppets of the Marathas. They also gave him the title of Amir-ul-Umara (head of Amirs) which means Supreme Commander.

Thus, Delhi came under the control of the Great Grand Maratha – as Mahadji Shinde was often called. He was also known as Mahadji Scindia, and his ensign, the saffron Nagnishani or Serpent Standard was proudly raised on the Red Fort and havelis all over the city of Delhi.

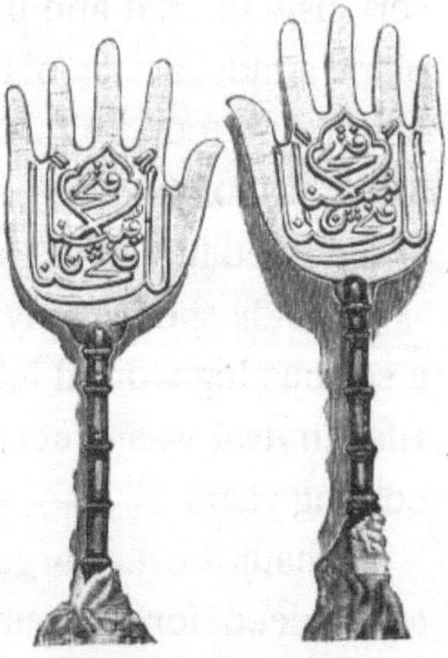

The Badshahi *Panja*: a dignity conferred on Mahadji Shinde by the Mughal emperor

His extensive conquests in north India had made him a most powerful figure. He seized Gwalior from the Jats and served as the Raja of Gwalior for over 25 years till his death. Gwalior became the leading state in the

The Maratha court

Maratha Confederacy, and one of the foremost military powers in India.

Mahadji was a capable and wise administrator who disciplined his army, making it proficient with modern arms and artillery. He also issued and minted various coins. Throughout his life he reconstructed several places of worship all over India. He also patronized religious places, irrespective of their faith.

An important initiative that he took was to combine the forces of the Mughals, Marathas, Jats, Sikhs and Rajputs into his army called Fauj-e-Hind, against the might of the British. This rainbow coalition fought under the Scindia flag to defeat the British many times.

The Marathas ruled Delhi from 1757–1803 with a break from 1761–71. They eventually lost to the British East India Company in the Second Anglo-Maratha War (1803-1805). This resulted in major losses of territory including the Delhi region for the Marathas.

Mahadji dreamt of a united country and fought for self-rule for India. He is remembered for his struggle to establish Hindavi Swarajya, the precursor to Indian nationalism. The English historian Henry George Keene, who wrote a book about Mahadji Shinde, is believed to have said that among Asian luminaries of the time, there was no man to match Mahadji.

Timeline:
1747–1859 CE

11

The British Come... and Stay

From Trade to Territory

Nadir Shah's invasion of India had probably led the British East India Company to recognize the weakness of the tottering Mughal Empire, and it paved their way to enter India to fill the power vacuum. They stayed on here to subjugate and rule the entire country.

A trading company, the English East India Company first came to India during the reign of the Mughal emperor Jahangir to break the Dutch monopoly over the spice trade. The Dutch were among the first Europeans to arrive in India, setting foot on the subcontinent as traders in the early seventeenth century. By the middle of the eighteenth century they had the strongest trading presence, with major outposts in Calcutta, Bombay and Bengal. They had become masters of the pepper trade, making huge profits by selling the Black Gold, as it was called, in Europe. Later, cleverly taking advantage of the prevailing anarchy, the English East India Company slowly but surely increased its powers to gain control over large parts of the country, leading to the decline of the Dutch.

The nawab of Bengal, Siraj-ud-Daulah, had given the East India Company several trade concessions, which were misused by its employees to carry on their private trade. They had also formed close links with the business community and big bankers of Murshidabad, the capital of Bengal, who gave them financial support. When the nawab decided to take firm action against the company, a conspiracy was hatched against him, leading to the momentous Battle of Plassey in 1757. The young Siraj was seen as a powerful deterrent to the expansion of British rule in India.

A treacherous betrayal by Mir Jafar, the commander of Siraj-ud-Daulah's forces, proved a turning point in the history of India, for the battle was decisive in cementing the British foothold here. The British presence in Bengal and their access to its great wealth now made it possible for them to expand their empire rapidly to the rest of the country.

The British acquired Delhi in 1803 when they defeated the Maratha forces after the Second Anglo-Maratha War, ending Maratha rule over the city. And so the destinies of the old city underwent a change again! It now came under the control of the East India Company, and became a part of the north-western provinces. The British installed a 'Resident' at the court in the Red Fort, and the Mughal emperor, Shah Alam II, remained a mere figurehead.

In fact, by the nineteenth century, the British had become the dominant political and military power in India. They were

The Battle of Assaye during the Second Anglo-Maratha War

soon able to push out other colonial powers like the French and the Dutch to establish their undisputed authority in the subcontinent.

Several Indian rulers fought the British desperately, determined not to give up their kingdoms. Brave queens like Rani Chennamma of Kittur, Begum Hazrat Mahal of Awadh and Rani Lakshmibai of Jhansi took up arms against the British and set an example in courage. They knew that the company would annex their kingdoms in the absence of a male heir.

The 1857 War of Indian Independence was the first united Indian uprising. The unrest spread like wildfire everywhere, indicating the wide scale of discontent. Delhi became the focal point of the uprising as it was the seat of the old, though largely powerless, Mughal emperor. Over 1,00,000 troops marched into the city, rallying against the British forces, to ask for the support and leadership of emperor Bahadur Shah Zafar, which he reluctantly gave. Most rebelling Indian kings had agreed to unite under the banner of the Mughal emperor till the British were defeated.

For four months, there was widespread killing of the British by Indian troops. This was followed by looting and a severe food crisis. The British now gathered a huge mercenary army and began retaliatory killings. Delhi occupied a key strategic position between Calcutta and the new territories of Punjab. Therefore, its recapture was important for the British.

The gates of Delhi were closed and there was a bloody massacre in the city. Much of it was destroyed, once again. The Mughal emperor was arrested and exiled to Burma. It was the end of over three hundred years of Mughal rule!

The 1857 uprising was the biggest threat to British colonial power during its rule of almost two centuries. The violent struggle led to the end of East India Company rule in India, which had lasted a hundred years, up to 1858. It also marked the beginning of the long struggle for independence from British colonial rule. After the events of the War of Independence, the

British Crown assumed direct administration of India in the new British colony.

However, in 1859, the very next year after the takeover by the Crown, Calcutta was made the capital of the British Raj, in a move to punish Delhi for being the centre of the uprising. And it remained so till the early twentieth century. Delhi fell into the deep shadow of neglect once again.

Meanwhile, the British annexed many princely states, forming laws and policies of their own. They managed to divide the people and gain power, and the entire Indian subcontinent came rapidly under their control. Ruthless repression, excesses committed by British soldiers and a plague epidemic only added to the misery of the public.

The story of British colonization in India is one of oppression and economic exploitation of the vast country and its people. Two hundred years of British rule tragically reduced India from its glory of being one of the world's richest countries to among the very poorest. And despite our ancient expertise in almost every sphere - from metallurgy and shipbuilding to agriculture and textiles, colonial repression of indigenous production made India almost totally dependent on foreign imports.

The spirit of revolt that was lit in 1857 led eventually to a great awakening everywhere, and the first beginnings of Indian nationalism. One day, the dream of an unfettered and free India would come true!

The Last Mughal Emperor

Not the light of anyone's eyes,
Nor solace for anyone's heart,
Of no use to anyone,
I am that one fistful of dust...

- Bahadur Shah Zafar

The tragic figure of Bahadur Shah Zafar, India's last Mughal emperor, presided over a Mughal Empire that extended barely beyond Delhi's Red Fort.

After the British take-over of the city in 1803, the Mughal rulers in Delhi, Shah Alam ll, Akbar Shah ll and finally Bahadur Shah Zafar, were treated with some respect by the British East India Company, but they were mere figureheads. Bahadur Shah had been reduced to a state of complete dependence. He was paid a meagre pension and allowed to collect some taxes. He could also maintain a token military force in Delhi. The British maintained that he was the sovereign, but they well knew that he posed no threat to anybody.

Bahadur Shah Zafar himself had little interest in statecraft and did not possess any imperial ambitions. A mystical Sufi thinker, he was widely regarded as a saint and teacher. Also, a poet at heart, he had penned many great ghazals in Urdu, the language of the elite, like the one at the beginning of this chapter. In one of his verses, Zafar stated that both Hinduism and Islam shared the same essence. His court thus embodied a fusion of Hindu and Islamic cultures. It was home to several eminent Urdu poets like Zauq, Mirza Ghalib and Momin, and was alive with its *mushairas* or poetry reading sessions.

Bahadur Shah Zafar

With the rapid spread of the 1857 War of Independence, Hindus and Muslims alike sought a figure that could unite all Indians. And who could be more acceptable as the Emperor of India than Zafar? Most rebelling Indian kings agreed to unite under *Shahenshah-e-Hind* Bahadur Shah Zafar until the British were defeated.

The old emperor accepted the leadership of the uprising against the mighty British with the utmost reluctance. After all, he was eighty-two years old and in the sunset of his life. He only wished for a life of peace and seclusion.

However, the war of independence, which started in Meerut a hundred kilometres away, was spreading like a conflagration, indicating widespread resentment against the British rulers. Almost the entire northern Gangetic plain rose up as one. Within four months, over 1,00,000 troops had marched into Delhi under the banner of the Mughal emperor, against their common foe. Despite the troubled situation, it was a time of complete communal harmony.

There was widespread killing of the British by the Indian troops in Delhi. Without the direction of a strong leader, they started becoming unruly and even took to looting. As a severe food crisis set in, many soldiers also began to disperse.

The old emperor imposed stiff punishments to control Delhi's declining law and order situation. He also tried to stop the killing of innocent Europeans, even sheltering them in his palace.

However, the British soon gained the upper hand as they gathered a vast mercenary army and retaliated. Bahadur Shah took refuge in Humayun's Tomb on the outskirts of Delhi, along with his wife, Zeenat Mahal, two sons, Mirza Mughal and Mirza Khizr Sultan, and a grandson, Mirza Abu Bakr. It was not long before British forces led by Major William Hodson surrounded the tomb and forced him to surrender.

The next day, William Hodson procured an unconditional surrender from the three princes hiding at Humayun's Tomb. On their way to the Red Fort, Hodson abruptly ordered the three to get down at an archway called Lal Darwaza, near Delhi Gate. He shot them dead at point blank range and declared Delhi's capture. The bodies were displayed in front of the *kotwali* (police station). The archway came to be called Khooni Darwaza ('bloody gate') on today's Bahadur Shah Zafar Marg.

Delhi mapped before the siege of Delhi in 1858

…ak. 8. Canal-street. 9. The Banking-house. 10. The Jumma Musjid. 11. The Sadoola Khan. 12. The Musjid Fetipore. 13. [illegible] Gate. 14. Cashmere Gate. 15. English Church. 16. Magazine and Store Houses. 17. Skinner's House. 18. Custom House. 19. Martello Towers. 20. Kotab [illegible]. 21. Ruins of Ancient Delhi.

…RE THE SIEGE

The last Mughal Emperor surrenders to Major William Hodson

Delhi was now destined for another massacre. Its gates were closed, and the British forces ordered their troops to shoot at sight. Much of the city, its precious monuments and gardens were wantonly destroyed, and replaced with unsightly army barracks. Manuscripts were burned, and treasures in art, sculpture, gems and jewellery were stolen and sent to Britain.

The British forces killed or imprisoned the surviving members of the Mughal dynasty. After a speedy 'trial' at the Red Fort, which he had once commanded, Bahadur Shah Zafar himself was arrested and exiled to Rangoon in Burma (now Yangon in the Union of Myanmar)

Tucked away in Mehrauli, Zafar Mahal, once the summer retreat of Bahadur Shah, now stands in ruins. Intended to be his final resting place where he had identified a spot for his grave, the palace served as the backdrop for the Phoolwalon Ki Sair that would once start from here.

in 1858. His wife and a few survivors of his family went with him. His departure marked the unceremonious end of more than three centuries of Mughal rule in India. It was the end of an era.

Bahadur Shah died in exile in 1862. In a marble enclosure adjoining the *dargah* of the great Sufi saint, Qutbuddin Bakhtiyar Kaki at Mehrauli, an empty site marks the grave where he had willed to be buried alongside some of his Mughal predecessors. Sadly, this was never to be so, as he wrote poignantly as a British captive in Rangoon –

How unlucky is Zafar!
For his burial
Not even two yards of earth
Are to be had in the land of his beloved!

While part of the poetic work of Bahadur Shah Zafar was lost or destroyed during the War of Independence in 1857, a large collection survived and was later compiled into the *Kulliyyat-i-Zafar*. His Urdu poetry continues to be admired, and his ghazals are sung to this day.

From time to time, the issue of bringing back the remains of the Sufi poet-emperor to Delhi from the shrine in Yangon has been raised. Delhi remembers its reluctant leader of India's first War of Independence with a major road named after him. Bahadur Shah Zafar Marg in central Delhi, sometimes referred to as the 'Fleet Street of India', is dotted with several newspaper offices. The name of this road serves to remind us of India's last Mughal emperor, and of perhaps one of the most tumultuous periods of Delhi's history.

Mirza Ghalib and the City He Loved

One of Delhi's most loved poets, Mirza Beg Asadullah Khan, better known as Mirza Ghalib, was part of the imperial court of Bahadur Shah Zafar. He wrote in both Urdu and Persian. The emperor conferred several titles on him and appointed him the royal historian of the Mughal Court as also poet-tutor to the royal family. This incorporated him into the nobility of Delhi, the city he cherished.

He immortalized Delhi when he wrote, *I asked my soul, 'What is Delhi?' It replied, 'The world is the body and Delhi its soul.'* And along with the old city, he loved its gastronomic delights: roast mutton, kebabs, dal, *sohan* halwa and yes, mangoes!

Of course there is a Ghalib-related anecdote of the mango season. The city was flooded with luscious mangoes. The emperor was strolling in a mango orchard at the Red Fort, full of laden trees, along with some companions. He noticed Mirza Ghalib staring closely at a few overhanging mangoes. The emperor asked curiously, 'Mirza, what are you looking at so attentively?'

Ghalib replied with folded hands that he had heard that every fruit has the name of its destined eater and ancestors written on it. So he was trying to see if his name or that of any of his ancestors was written on any of the mangoes. The emperor smiled widely, and that very same day had baskets full of the finest mangoes sent to the poet!

Knowing of Ghalib's great fondness for mangoes, people everywhere sent him gifts of mangoes. But they were never enough! He would go on to buy more in the local bazaar. Once his friends were discussing the merits of mangoes. When asked for his opinion, he replied unhesitatingly that only two things were important – that the mangoes were sweet and they were plentiful!

Mirza Ghalib

He was sitting with his friends when a donkey came and sniffed at a fallen mango and some peels on the ground, before ambling away. His friends observed that *even* donkeys didn't eat mangoes! Ghalib retorted in his witty way that *only* donkeys didn't eat mangoes!

Mirza Ghalib was barely eleven years old when he started composing poetry! Although his first language was Urdu, he was well versed in Persian and Turkish, which were spoken at home. He became well known for his verses and ghazals on many subjects like philosophy, the troubles of life and its mysteries. He was also a gifted and witty letter writer.

His personal life was not a happy one, although he never really worked for a living, depending on royal patronage or the generosity of his friends. He lived to see the eclipse of the mighty Mughal Empire and its last emperor deposed, the rise of the English East India Company rule, and the Indian War of Independence, all of which shattered his dreams. As he witnessed gruesome events unfold in his beloved city, he described them in his work. He saw bazaars, lanes and localities disappear, and friends' havelis razed to the ground. He lamented that Delhi was tragically transformed from being a thriving metropolis to a desert, and a military camp –

'*Five things kept Delhi alive – the Red Fort, Chandni Chowk, the daily crowds at the Jama Masjid, the weekly walk to the Yamuna Bridge and the annual fair of flower-sellers. These five things are no more. Where is Delhi now? Yes, there used to be a city of this name in the land of Hindustan.*'

His haveli in Chandni Chowk's Ballimaran is said to have been presented to him by an admirer, a *hakim*. Mirza Ghalib lived here for a long time till his death, and wrote some of his finest poetry and ghazals here. Many have since, been sung and immortalized. Known as Ghalib Ki Haveli, this 300-year-old heritage site has been turned into a 'Ghalib Memorial' today, and houses a permanent Ghalib exhibition, in memory of the city's legendary poet.

Delhi's Oldest Church

James Skinner lay wounded on the battlefield in Uniara in Rajasthan, groaning in pain. He had been shot in the groin and had lain there for over twenty-four hours, considered dead. He thought to himself, 'If I get out of here alive, I vow to build a church...'

Fondly known as 'Sikandar Sahib' by the soldiers who served under him, Colonel James Skinner was an Anglo-Indian military adventurer with a Rajput mother and a Scottish father, Hercules Skinner, who was a soldier in the East India Company. Young James was unable to serve as an officer here because of his mixed parentage. So he enlisted instead in the Maratha army, where he served under Gwalior's Maharaja Scindia for eight years, showing shrewd military talent. He quickly rose in the ranks to become commander-in-chief, remaining loyal to the Scindia during the Anglo-Maratha wars. However, he was dismissed from the Maratha army eventually, along with other Anglo-Indians, because of their mixed blood.

Colonel James Skinner

He joined the Bengal Army of the East India Company, who now took him in, and established a cavalry regiment called Skinner's Horse or 'The Yellow Boys' – because of the bright yellow colour of their uniform. This regiment came to be renowned in the British Indian Army for its expertise with horses and weapons, and is still a part of the Indian Army. But James Skinner had one condition – that he would never be made to fight his former master, the Maharaja Scindia.

He also never forgot the vow he made in 1800 on the battlefield of Uniara. That is how Delhi's oldest church, St. James' Church, also known as Skinner's Church, came to be built in Kashmiri

St. James' Church, Kashmiri Gate

Gate, at his own expense, a small fortune of 95,000 rupees, between 1826 and 1836. Designed by Major Robert Smith, the elegant church stands on a cruciform plan (Greek Cross) with three porticoed porches, elaborate stained-glass windows and a central octagonal dome. It became the official church of the viceroys of India who attended services here right till 1931.

After that, the Cathedral Church of the Redemption, also known as the Viceroy Church, was built east of Parliament House and the regal Viceroy's House. This magnificent church was then used for prayers by later viceroys.

James Skinner is also said to have built a temple and a mosque for his fourteen wives. He was buried with full military honours in a vault of white marble, beneath the altar of the church he had built. It was badly damaged during the 1857 War of Independence by rebels, and its early records and books were destroyed. Later, a giant cross in memory of the British and Christians killed at the church and in Delhi, was erected in the church garden. It stands here even today. The church has been restored recently, and is a well-maintained heritage building and an important religious centre, especially during festivals such as Christmas, Palm Sunday and Easter. Its sprawling lawns also host marriages, baptism and other ceremonies.

Colonel James Skinner was proficient in Persian and wrote a volume of memoirs of his military expeditions in Persian, with biographies of Sikh and Rajput princely families. He was an important patron of the arts, and his intimate knowledge of the Indian people made governor generals and commanders-in-chief seek his advice at all times.

Commemorative stamp issued in 1978 by the Government of India on the 175th Anniversary of Skinner's Horse

He is sometimes referred to as the 'father of the Indian cavalry'. The historian, Mildred Archer, said of Skinner: 'Among military adventurers who have served in India, none was more dashing than the half-Indian leader of the famous Irregular Cavalry Corps known as Skinner's Horse.'

Timeline:
1884 CE–Today

12

The Eighth City
India's Capital: New Delhi

A New Delhi

Those were bittersweet years leading up to the twentieth century. The spark of nationalism that had been lit eventually paved the way for the formation of the Indian National Congress in 1885. It was a new beginning, for this was a platform for civil and political dialogue and appeal between educated Indians and the British government.

The British on the other hand, tried to cement their power over the Indians with symbols of imperial power and even splendour. As a start, the Indian army and the finances of the Indian administration were reorganized extensively.

The Delhi Durbar of 1911 was perhaps the grandest extravaganza of the British Raj. Held in north Delhi's Coronation Park, all the rajas and nawabs of the princely states of India were summoned in full regal finery to mark the coronation of King George V as the Emperor of India. At this grand event, the King made a crucial announcement. He proclaimed that the British had decided to shift their capital from Calcutta to a site near the ancient capital of Delhi. The old city would reclaim its lost status! What is now known as the eighth city of Delhi was thus built by the British between 1911 and 1922.

The new capital, named 'New Delhi' by a Government of India notification in 1926, was to be the 'jewel in the Crown'. Envisioned as the imperial capital of the largest colony of the British Empire, it was to convey the idea of colonial magnificence and might.

The Delhi Durbar, 1911

This grand capital was constructed at a site west of the historic Purana Qila, around Raisina Hill, five kilometres south of the old city of Delhi, with ample scope for expansion. The young city – a spacious metropolis with wide, tree-lined avenues, was designed by English architects Sir Edwin Lutyens and Herbert Baker to be a worthy successor to its ancient heritage. It was a classic combination of western architecture and traditional Indian features, and was developed in a geometric design, mainly with hexagons and triangles.

Lutyens laid out the city's central administrative area. At its heart was constructed the magnificent 340-room Viceroy's House on the top of Raisina Hill, which looked down on the majestic King's Way, with its sprawling lush lawns, majestic trees and Boat Club. King's Way was so named in honour of King George V's visit to the city for the Delhi Durbar. There were sprawling lawns and canals on both sides, and carefully chosen trees were planted along the avenues for shade in the stifling summer heat.

The famous Mughal Gardens, designed by Lutyens and Mustoe in 1928, extended over fifteen acres of the viceregal estate. They drew inspiration from the Mughal Gardens of Jammu and

Kashmir as well as the English flower garden. Masses of flowers were laid amidst the geometric beds, canals and terraces of Mughal design, and blended artistically with European-style flower beds, lawns and hedges.

Near at hand stood the stately circular Parliament House, designed by Herbert Baker, and inaugurated in 1927 by Lord Irwin, the Governor General of India. The Secretariat Building was designed by Herbert Baker as well.

At one end of King's Way was erected one of the most iconic national monuments of India, the World War I Memorial, India Gate, designed by Lutyens. The names of 90,000 Indian soldiers martyred during the First World War and the Third Anglo-Afghan War, are inscribed on this imposing 42-metre-high gateway, constructed with pale stone, red stone and granite.

And that was not all. Other architects designed buildings such as the Anglican and Catholic cathedrals near the Viceroy's House. Connaught Place, now Rajiv Chowk, was planned in concentric circles as a spacious commercial centre, with elegant white colonnades and covered walkways, in the Georgian style of architecture. It is difficult to imagine that this main high-end shopping and business district of New Delhi, designed for the elite living in Lutyens Delhi Bungalow Zone, was once a ridge covered with thorny scrub and *kikar* trees, and inhabited by jackals and wild pigs! Once upon a time, it is said, residents of Kashmiri Gate and the Civil Lines areas would come here during weekends for partridge hunting.

Rajiv Chowk's Central Park has one of India's largest national flags, measuring a staggering 90 feet x 60 feet at the top of a 207-foot mast. When it was hoisted here in March 2014, it was the biggest tricolour in the world!

Thus, as the city of Delhi recovered from the fiery 1857 uprising, its very character seemed to have changed. The most prominent buildings constructed here, like the Parliament House and the regal Viceroy's House, served as prestigious symbols of British rule.

All this while, revolutionary activities in Delhi continued unabated as the spirit of nationalism intensified. The government responded with lathi charges, ruthless suppression and atrocities. The outbreak of the First World War in 1914 brought new hardships for the people, with no sign of reforms. They had to face food shortages, rising prices, heavy taxation and unemployment.

It was at such a time of upheaval in India that Mohandas Karamchand Gandhi came onto the scene, after his heroic struggle against oppression in South Africa. Through Ahimsa and Satyagraha or 'truth force', he taught Indians to stand fearlessly for their rights while shunning violence.

The people of Delhi responded enthusiastically to Gandhiji's call for non-cooperation against the British government. 'Swaraj' was the new cry! Thousands followed the call to dedicate themselves wholly to the service of the enslaved motherland. As the city saw mass rallies, strikes and civil disobedience, a mood of defiance began to replace submission to British rule.

The government tried desperately to curb this spirit with repressive measures. Thousands perished facing bullets and in prisons, many of them unknown and unsung. The countrywide civil disobedience and non-cooperation movement were new weapons as the people resolved to win Poorna Swaraj from tyrannous British yoke.

Revolutionaries like Bhagat Singh and Batukeshwar Dutt threw bombs at the Central Legislative Assembly at Delhi, "to make the deaf hear," and to remind the government of its callous exploitation of the country. Bhagat Singh was hanged to death a couple of years later, along with freedom fighters Shivaram Rajguru and Sukhdev Thapar, for plotting to kill the police chief

Bhagat Singh

responsible for the death of Lala Lajpat Rai, during a silent protest march.

National movements like Gandhiji's Salt Satyagraha, a mass civil disobedience movement against the unjust salt tax imposed by the government, echoed strongly in Delhi, the seat of power. Gandhiji and eighty followers marched all the way to the coastal town of Dandi from Sabarmati Ashram in Gujarat to make salt from the sea. 'Gyarah Murti', a massive sculptural tribute in black stone stands in the heart of Delhi, depicting Gandhiji's salt march.

Critical years in the struggle for freedom followed, as Indians moved towards self-government. Anti-government agitation spread like wildfire with the 1942 Quit India movement, also known as August Kranti, demanding an end to British colonial

Mahatma Gandhi (centre) in Delhi in October 1939; to extreme left is Dr Rajendra Prasad, and to extreme right, Sardar Patel

rule. In Burma, Subhas Chandra Bose thundered in his iconic speech to the Indian National Army, 'Give me blood, and I promise you freedom!' It was the biggest mass struggle of the freedom movement, and almost the entire leadership of the Indian National Congress was arrested and taken to unknown destinations. Public anger erupted. Ordinary Indians from all walks of life took to the streets, even without the traditional leadership of the Congress.

Delhi saw mass protests, strikes and stray incidents of violence and damage to government property. Spontaneous demonstrations outside the Viceroy's House spread to colleges and schools, and academic activities were boycotted by Delhi University students who demanded the release of the national leaders. The British responded with brute force, swinging lathis and gagging of the press.

A call for 'Delhi Chalo' was one of the slogans used during the Quit India movement, urging protesters all over the country to march to Delhi and challenge British rule. The government again responded with a heavy-handed crackdown everywhere.

By the end of the Second World War, Britain realized that it could not hold on to India much longer. The Labour Prime Minister, Clement Attlee, declared that discussions would be held with Indian leaders regarding the country's Constitution and transfer of power to Indian hands. Freedom was in sight! An interim government was formed in 1946 under Jawaharlal Nehru with 12 members. Crucial negotiations and discussions in Delhi eventually led to the partition of India and the transfer of power from the British government to Indian leaders.

There had emerged a disturbing element on the scene, namely communal ill-will. Muhammad Ali Jinnah had declared Pakistan as the goal of his party, the Muslim League, which had been demanding separate representation and electorates. The problem of communalism could not be curbed, and horrifying riots rocked many places even as the country moved towards independence.

A resolution for the partition of the country was passed at the annual session of the Indian National Congress at Delhi in June 1947. Dr Rajendra Prasad, who was also the president of the Constituent Assembly, presided over this crucial session. Later, he would go on to become the first president of India.

Long years of blood, sweat and tears gave India her freedom at last, in August 1947. New Delhi became the capital of free India and the seat of government of the young republic!

Independence brought with it new hopes and dreams. The Indian tricolour was unfurled from the historic Red Fort for the first time by Jawaharlal Nehru, the first prime minister of free India. He gave his memorable 'Tryst with Destiny' speech on the eve of India's independence, in Parliament House, considered one of the greatest speeches of the twentieth century.

However, independence had a tragic price to pay, for with it came Partition, creating two countries from one, and uprooting people all over the subcontinent. It brought with it death and destruction as millions became homeless. Its reverberations were felt the most in the capital city as a massive influx of refugees from Pakistan changed the very fabric of the city's population. Delhi took in nearly half a million refugees in those brutal months, almost doubling the population of the city. All planning for the national capital was thrown completely out of gear!

The new refugees stayed in camps in parks, schools, military barracks and even historical monuments, mosques and temples, hoping to build themselves new homes. The Begumpuri Masjid, the Purana Qila and the neighbouring Humayun's Tomb became vast sites for refugee camps. The very map of the city now changed as its boundaries expanded in all directions.

Less than six months after Partition, Mahatma Gandhi, the Father of the Nation, tragically fell to an assassin's bullets here. Bapu, as he was fondly called, was on his way to a prayer meeting in the compound of Birla House in central Delhi, where he had been conducting multi-faith prayer meetings every evening. And so the twentieth century's most famous apostle of non-violence sadly met with a violent end himself.

Rebuilding lives from scratch in their new city of refuge, the industrious refugees enhanced trade and commerce in Delhi. They were joined by migrants from other Indian states, who came with stars in their eyes to this city of rainbow dreams. Opportunities opened as never before. The character of the once stately old city well known for its *tehzeeb* (or refinement), transformed beyond recognition, as it soon became a competitive place of enterprise and opportunity. Over the years, New Delhi came to be transformed by its people – just as they were by this vibrant city.

India became a Republic on 26 January 1950, and Dr Rajendra Prasad was sworn in as the first president of India. The Viceroy's House became the official residence of the president and came to be known as Rashtrapati Bhavan. Today, its splendid Mughal Gardens have been renamed Amrit Udyan, and are open to all visitors in the spring, when rare species of exotic flowers from all over the world – tulips, orchids, cherry blossoms, water lilies and many others bloom in a riot of colours amid fountains.

The Central Vista, running from Rashtrapati Bhavan to India Gate, was given its Hindi name of Rajpath after independence. This distinctive stretch where the might of India's armed forces is on display every Republic Day since 1950, has been now renamed for the third time as Kartavya Path. While Rajpath symbolized the power of the British Raj, Kartavya Path represents the spirit of public empowerment and a sense of duty. The popular

The majestic Rashtrapati Bhavan

greens around have been redesigned with pedestrian walkways, sandstone fixtures, underpasses and bridges over the canals.

Situated in the heart of New Delhi, India Gate came to symbolize the city and its identity, attracting hordes of visitors and picnickers every day. After the Bangladesh liberation war of 1971, India Gate housed the Amar Jawan Jyoti or 'eternal flame' that honoured the gallant unknown soldier killed in the defence of the country. Symbolized by an inverted bayonet capped by a war helmet, the Amar Jawan Jyoti burning beside it was manned round the clock by soldiers from the three services of the Indian armed forces. The prime minister of India customarily pays tribute to the fallen soldiers at this site along with the heads of the Indian Armed Forces, before the beginning of the annual Republic Day parade held at Rajpath, the ceremonial boulevard of the capital of India.

The Amar Jawan Jyoti has since been moved to a new destination, the National War Memorial, spread over 40 acres of land near the India Gate canopy. This elegant national monument has been built in memory of soldiers of the Indian forces who fought in armed conflicts of independent India. The names of those killed are inscribed on the memorial walls in golden letters. The memorial is now the site for the president and the prime minister of India to place wreaths and pay tribute to the Indian defence forces.

Visitors may now walk under the India Gate arch towards the India Gate canopy. Under this canopy, where the statue of King George V once stood, a 28-foot-tall statue of Netaji Subhas Chandra Bose, the revolutionary leader of the freedom struggle, has been installed.

New Delhi's imposing India Gate

The reconstruction of the Central Vista and the central administrative area around Raisina Hill to house new ministerial buildings, a new Parliament House, and restored monuments and parks, are all recent transformations of the city. The National Museum and the National Gallery of Modern Art stand close by with their timeless treasures. The sprawling Pragati Maidan trade fair complex has been redeveloped into a cultural hub with meeting rooms, auditoriums, halls and a huge amphitheatre.

New Delhi is perhaps the world's oldest capital city if one were to consider Yudhishthira's splendid Indraprastha. Indeed, few places in the world are so steeped in history! And no matter however many names it may have acquired over the ages, Delhi with its unbroken ancient traditions and rich culture, has always been intrinsically identified with pomp, power and imperial sway.

However, the city pays a heavy price today for its mushrooming population, rapid expansion and development. Climate change, congestion, noise and traffic nightmares are the grim realities its people face today, although they have always contended with scorching summers and bone-chilling winters. Situated in the arid belt near the Rajasthan desert, the Delhi region in recent times has often been inundated during the wet monsoon months. Its glorious winter sun is now commonly blotted out by an alarming haze of pollution, that can turn into a lethal cocktail. And as toxic contamination chokes the Yamuna, the city's eternal lifeline threatens to become little more than moving sludge.

Yet the majestic old trees of Delhi, the flaming *gulmohur*, the golden laburnum and the violet jacaranda still burst into glorious colour with the onset of summer. Bright winter flowers bedeck the city's many roundabouts; the bulbul calls and the koel sings, igniting a million dreams with the change of seasons.

And so the spirit of Delhi lives on...

And that is indeed the magic of the eternal city!

The Yamuna: Till Eternity

I AM YAMUNA, born of the mighty sun god Surya and the cloud goddess Sanjana. As a young maiden, I descended from the heavens to the Yamunotri Glacier on the Kalind Mountain of the lower Himalayas, to sanctify Mother Earth.

Long, long ago, I was called Yami, the goddess of life, and was my father's favourite child. Yama, the god of death, was my twin brother, and he was the first mortal on earth. I also came to be known as Kalindi, after the mountain I had come from. Perhaps this name came from my duskiness as well. My once clear waters had turned dark when Shiva jumped into my torrents, overcome with grief for his dead wife Sati.

Gushing down mountains and valleys, I reached the vast plains below, travelling almost 1,500 kilometres, till I merged with the holy waters of the Ganga and Saraswati at the venerated Triveni Sangam in Prayagraj.

My memories go back a long way to the time when Vasudev, the father of baby Krishna carried him to safety from his wicked uncle, Kansa. As I parted my turbulent waters to give them safe passage, I tried to touch the infant's feet, for I knew instantly that he was divine. I also remember the many-headed serpent Kaliya, who made my waters his abode. His venom killed many living beings, till I turned black as the night. Finally, he was defeated by the young Krishna and banished into the underworld, to my great relief.

Baby Krishna being carried across the Yamuna by Vasudeva

I flowed past the vast and arid Khandavaprastha forest where Indraprastha, Yudhisthira's splendid capital city, was created. I was blessed to hear many mystical melodies played by young Krishna on his flute, on my banks. Krishna was once visiting his cousins, the Pandavas, in Indraprastha, when they bathed in my clear waters. As a young maiden, I had performed many austerities on the banks in my goddess form, to win the hand of Vishnu, the master of all the worlds. Captivated by my beauty, Krishna agreed to Arjun's suggestion to marry me. He was, after all, the avatar of Vishnu. I recall how he took me in his chariot, first to the Indraprastha palace and then to Dwarka, where we were married.

Down the ages, I saw fortune seekers and kings, barbarians and commoners come to Delhi to seek their destinies. I saw the seven cities of Delhi all rise and crumble – and then arise again, in a thousand different ways. And all recognized that my abundant waters were enough to sustain their brand-new capital cities.

I saw emperors stride my sandy banks, sometimes solitary figures deeply furrowed in thought, and at other festive moments with their queens, princes and courtiers. Elephant fights, kite flying and festivals were celebrated on my banks amid much merriment. There came other sombre moments of mourning too. For thousands of years great seers meditated on my banks, and made their ashrams and shrines here. Their sanctity resonated with me, and I felt like the goddess I really was. And then there came all too often, periods of darkness and despair. But the spirit of the city always survived as valiant new heroes, the saviours of the land, rose to fight the oppressors.

When Shah Jahan moved his capital from Agra to Delhi, he sailed up the Yamuna, entering the newly built Red Fort through the Yamuna Gate or Khizri Darwaza. Ironically, Bahadur Shah Zafar escaped the Red Fort in 1857 through the same water gate. It was named after Khwaja Khizr, a Sindhi saint of the waters also known as Jhulelaal, revered by both Hindus and Muslims of Sindh.

And I, Yamuna, remained an inseparable part of these times.

With independence came industrialization and development. But my waters had muddied and I was being slowly choked to death. *Pollution!* Millions of litres of industrial effluents, untreated sewage, chemicals and waste water began to be discharged recklessly into my waters every day.

I, Yamuna, once worshipped over the centuries for my healing waters, have turned today into a dying river that sadly ceases to support aquatic life. And that is why my reeking waters flow

such a dark black. What is more, rampant construction on my floodplains has made me overflow my banks in Delhi, creating havoc, for thousands must be evacuated. My plight has made me an angry river indeed!

The city's alarming contamination of my waters poses an ominous threat to its own survival. Once the lifeline and cultural hub of Delhi, I must be saved before it is too late.

For I am Yamuna, the eternal witness to Delhi.

These are stories of Delhi of long long ago...stories that make history, mythology and legend. They have come to us down the ages, sometimes by word of mouth and at others through books, manuscripts and inscriptions, forming a part of our collective identity. A few may be difficult to verify as being historically true – but all these stories – as indeed stories within stories, make up the city's kaleidoscopic heritage.

Acknowledgements

My grateful thanks to Prof. Swadesh Chadha who retired as Associate Professor of History, Jesus and Mary College, University of Delhi, after a distinguished teaching career of 44 years including 20 years as head of the department – for making history so fascinating!

Image Copyright Information

Wikimedia Commons Public Domain License: x: Map adapted by Syed Salahuddin, based on *The Seven Cities*, 1906; author: Gordon Risley Hearn; https://en.wikisource.org/wiki/Page:The_Seven_Cities_of_Delhi.djvu/182; **12:** Ganga and Shatanu: Maharaja Fateh Singh Museum, Lakshmi Vilas Palace, Vadodara, Gujarat; Source/photographer: http://abhisays.com/art/selected-paintings-of-raja-ravi-varma-part-3.html; **23:** The Trial of the Princes, 1914; Source: https://en.wikisource.org/wiki/Page:Myths_of_the_Hindus_%26_Buddhists.djvu/167; Authors: Sister Nivedita and Ananda Kentish Coomaraswamy; Illustrator: Nandalal Bose; **31:** Muhammad Ghori: From Hutchinson's *Story of the Nations*; Source: https://archive.org/details/hutchinsonsstory00londuoft; **33:** Qutb Minar: Circa 1890; source: Leiden University Library, KITLV, image 377921 Collection Southeast Asian & Caribbean Images (KITLV); **35:** Leaf by Suma Begum from Vecteezy.com; **36:** Mughal 'Parchin kari' work: Source: Nemonoman (own work); **40:** Inscription on Iron Pillar: Source: Original photograph; Author: Photo by en:User:~shuri; **46:** Qutbuddin Bakhtiyar Kaki: Unknown date; Source: https://twitter.com/moomjamma/status/1077107107403624451; Unknown author; **51:** Razia Sultana: Circa 18th century; Unknown author; **52:** Razia Sultana: Circa 19th century; Author: Gulam Ali Khan; **54:** Jalaluddin Khilji: Source URL: http://blog.chughtaimuseum.com/?p=11309; Unknown date; Source: Blog website of Chughtai Museum, via: http://blog.chughtaimuseum.com; Unknown author; **55:** Rani Padmini of Chittor: Unknown author; Circa 1765; Bibliothèque nationale de France, Paris; Source/Photographer: http://expositions.bnf.fr /inde/grand/ exp_056.htm; **56:** Alauddin Khilji: Illustrated album leaf; late 17th century; Gift of Dr Julius Hoffman, 1909; source: https://www.metmuseum.org/ Collections/search-the-collections/ 445976?rpp=60&pg=27&ao=on&ft=india&pos=1612; **66**: Amir Khusro: Late 1600s or early 1700s; Source: Рукопись ИВ АН УзССР, 65, л. 68.; Author: Anonymous artist from Bokhara; 1500; **67:** Illustrated poem of Amir Khusro: Source: http://www.columbia.edu/itc/mealac/ pritchett/ 00routesdata/1200_1299/nizamuddin/amirkhusrau/amirkhusrau.html; Author: Amir Khusro; **70**: Ghiyasuddin Tughlak: Extraction from Shah Ghiyath al-Din Tughluq arrives in Tirhut by Muhammad Sadr Ala-i in his BasaUn al-uns, ca.1410; Istanbul, Topkapi Palace Museum Library, Ms. R.1032.jpg; **71:** Tughlakbad ruins: August 1949; Source: http://photodivision.gov.in/ writereaddata/ webimages/ thumbnails/ 10786.jpg; Author: Photo Division, Government of India; **72:** Tughlakabad Fort: Wikisource: from The Seven Cities of Delhi (1906) by Gordon Risley Hearn; **77:** Baba Farid: Unknown date; Source: https://twitter.com/ moomjamma/status/1077107107403624451; Unknown author; **89:** Muhammad bin Tughlak: Source: Hutchinson's Story of the Nations; Unknown author; **97:** Firoz Shah Kotla: by Thomas Daniell; Accession number: X768/2(11); British Library Asia, Pacific and Africa Collections; Source: https://www.bl.uk/onlinegallery/onlineex/ apac/other/ 019xzz000007682u00011000.html; **98–99:** Firoz Shah Kotla view:12 March 1937; Source: Memoirs of the Archaeological Survey of India no.52; Author: Archaeological Survey of India; **101:** Remains at Firoz Shah Kotla: by Thomas Daniell; British Library Asia, Pacific and Africa Collections; Source: https://www.bl.uk/onlinegallery/onlineex/apac/other/019xzz000004321u00007000.html#:~:text=The%20citadel%20(Daniell's%20Cotilla%20or,south%2Deast%20of%20modern%20Delhi; **112:** Timur: August 2008; Author: user:shako (own work); **114:** Timur: The Minneapolis Institute of Arts, 2014.101; date: between 1595 and 1600; Source: Imperial Library of Emperor Akbar; Author: *Zafarnama* of Sharaf Al-Din 'Ali Yazdi; **117**: Guru Nanak: Fresco at Bauli Sahib; Circa 19th century; Source: https://sikhhistory.quora.com/The-lives-of-the-first-5-Gurus-according-to-me-Life-of-Guru-Nanak-Shah-Ji-The-life-of-Guru-Nanak-is-according-to-the-m?comment_id=10003768&comment_type=3 (initial upload); **129:** Babur and Humayun: 650; Source: http://www.harekrsna.com/sun/features/05-10/features1731.htm; Unknown author; **134:** Calligraphy of a Quatrain: Cleveland Museum of Art, Indian and South East Asian Art, Accession number 2013.342.b; Gift in honour of Madeline Neves Clapp; Gift of Mrs. Henry White Cannon by exchange; Bequest of Louise T. Cooper; Leonard C. Hanna Jr. Fund; From the Catherine and Ralph Benkaim Collection; Source: https://clevelandart.

org/art/2013.342.b **138:** British crown: Source: G. Younghusband; C. Davenport (1919). The Crown Jewels of England. London: Cassell & Co. p. 18. (published in the US by Funk & Wagnalls, NY); Author: Cyril James Humphries Davenport (1848–1941); **139:** Hamida Banu Begum: Circa late 19th century; unknown artist; Source: http://www.indianminiaturepaintings.co.uk/Lucknow_Hamida-Banu-Begum_000495.html; **142:** Mir Sayyid Ali: 1555–56; Los Angeles County Museum of Art; Accession number: M.90.141.1 **145:** Hemu: 1910; Source: Hindustani Raj; Unknown author; **147:** Abdul Rahim Khan-i-Khanan: Extraction; Circa 1627; Source: https://asia.si.edu/object/F1939.50a/#object-content; Author: Hashim; **151:** Shahjahan: Circa 1628 or later; Source: http://www.columbia.edu/itc/mealac/pritchett/00routesdata/1600_1699/shahjahan/drawings/drawings.htm; **154–55:** Red Fort: Circa: 1852–54; artist: Ghulam Ali Khan **158:** Jantar Mantar: Extraction; by Thomas Daniell and William Daniell; 1808; **162:** Dara Shikoh: Unknown author; **163:** Aurangzeb: Extraction from Estampes par Nicolas de Larmessin.f153; Gallica Digital Library, digital ID btv1b84543563; **166:** Guru Har Krishan: late 17th century; Source: Social media account of Sial Mirza Goraya, URL: https://www.instagram.com/sialmirza.goraya/; Unknown author; **171:** Guru Gobind Singh: Circa 1800; Government Museum and Art Gallery, Chandigarh; Source: http://www.sikharts.com/art_2007_paintings. Html; Author: from the family workshop of Nainsukh of Guier; **175:** Nadir Shah: Circa 1740; Source: https://imagesonline.bl.uk/asset/143693; Per x of the *The Contest for Rule in Eighteenth-Century Iran: Idea of Iran* Vol. 11; unknown author; **178:** Shah Alam II: Source: https://www.sothebys.com/en/auctions/ecatalogue/2011/c-welch-part-ii-l11227/lot.150.html **184:** Mahadji Shinde: by James Wales; **184:** Badshahi Panja: Source: *Itihasa Samgraha* by Parasanis, Dattatraya Balavant Publication, 1908; https://archive.org/details/dli.ministry.28945/; **185:** Maratha court: Durbar hall, Maratha school, c. 1820; Source: A Second Paradise: Indian Courtly Life 1590-1947, by Naveen Patnaik (New York: Metropolitan Museum, 1985), p. 113; **189:** Battle of Assaye: Joseph Constantine Stadler (1755–1828) engraving after painting of William Heath (–1840); 1815; Collection, Source: National Army Museum, London; **192:** Bahadur Shah Zafar: Circa 1850; Unknown author; **194–95:** Delhi before siege of 1858: *The Illustrated London News* Jan 16, 1858; Source: Scan sourced from DELHI, 1857 (1858) provided by Prof. Emerita Frances Pritchett, Columbia University in Sept 2013 and used with permission from FP. Original source in public domain; Unknown author; **200:** Colonel James Skinner: 1836; Unknown artist; https://collection.nam.ac.uk/detail.php?acc=1956-02-622; National Army Museum, London; **201:** St. James' Church: 1858; Author: Harriet Christina Tytler; Source: http://www.bl.uk/onlinegallery/onlineex/apac/photocoll/n/019pho000000032u00003000.html; **205:** Delhi Durbar: 12 December 1911; Source: Scanned print obtained by the uploader via a seller on ebay.com; Unknown photographer; **208:** Bhagat Singh: April 1929; Source: Unknown author (Ramnath Photographers, Delhi); Mahatma Gandhi in Delhi: 2 October 1939; Author: Central Press; Source: https://www.architecturaldigest.in/content/gandhi-jayanti-iconic-photos-mahatma/; **216:** Vasudeva and Krishna: mid-18th century; Collection, Los Angeles County Museum of Art.

Other Licenses: 60: Gold coins: Wikimedia Commons: Creative Commons Attribution-Share Alike 2.5 Generic license; **Attribution:** Classical Numismatic Group, Inc. http://www.cngcoins.com; **104:** Topara pillar: Wikimedia Commons: Creative Commons Attribution-Share Alike 3.0 Unported license; Extraction; 14th century drawing from Sirat i-Firuz Shahi Author: Aditya somani; **105:** inscriptions on Topara pillar: Wikimedia Commons: Creative Commons Attribution-Share Alike 3.0 Unported license; extraction; author: Dhamijalok; **152:** Chandni Chowk: 1826 (c); Lithograph by Captain John Luard (1790–1875); published by C. Hullmandel, J. Graf and Soret, 1838 (c); NAM Accession Number: NAM. 1971-02-33-529-17; Copyright/Ownership, London; National Army Museum, London; Out of Copyright; **153:** Jama Masjid, Delhi: Courtesy of photographer Ashok Mathur; ©Ashok Mathur; **156:** Shri Digambar Jain Mandir, Delhi: Courtesy of photographer Ashok Mathur; ©Ashok Mathur; **202:** Skinner's Horse stamp: Wikimedia Commons Government Open Data License - India (GODL); 1978; Author: Post of India; Source: https://colnect.com/en/stamps/stamp/327435-175th_Anniv_Skinners_Horse_1803-1978-Anniversaries_-_Military-India.